ANOTHER CITY IS POSSIBLE WITH PARTICIPATORY BUDGETING

Montréal/New York/London

ANOTHER CITY IS POSSIBLE WITH PARTICIPATORY BUDGETING

Yves Cabannes, Editor

Foreword by Anne Hidalgo, Mayor of Paris

Black Rose Books No. RR386
Library and Archives Canada Cataloguing in Publication

Another city is possible with participatory budgeting / Yves Cabannes (ed);
Foreword, Anne Hidalgo, The Mayor of Paris.

Includes bibliographical references.
Issued in print and electronic formats.
ISBN 978-1-55164-640-4 (Paperback)
ISBN 978-1-55164-642-8 (Hardcover)
ISBN 978-1-55164-599-5 (Ebook)

1. Municipal finance--Case studies. 2. Finance, Public--Case studies.
Cabannes, Yves, editor

HJ9105.A56 2017   336'.014   C2017-900644-4   C2017-900645-2

C.P 35788 Succ. Léo Pariseau
Montréal, QC H2x 0A4
Canada
www.blackrosebooks.com

ORDERING INFORMATON

NORTH AMERICA & INTERNATIONAL

University of Toronto Press
5201 Dufferin Street
Toronto M3h 5T8
Canada
1(800) 565-9523 (Toll Free)
utpbooks@utpress.utoronto.ca

UK & EUROPE

Central Books
Freshwater Road
Dagenham RM8 1RX
England
+44(0)20 8525 8800
order@centralbooks.co.uk

Black Rose Books is the publishing project of Cercle Noir et Rouge

Acknowledgements

We extend our gratitude to Julien Woessner for his insightful comments all through the process, to all contributors mentioned in the different briefings and to each one of the cities and grassroots movements with whom this book was prepared. We acknowledge the support provided by the Charles Leopold Mayer Foundation for the original dossier published in 2015.

Credits

Coordinator of the series and book editor
Cabannes, Yves

Authors
Indicated in each one of the files

Translators into English
Richard Huber [from Portuguese and Spanish];
Alana Quintyle [from French];
Ming Zhuang [from Chinese];
Chantal Coutu and Andrée Deveault [Foreword translation from French]

Editing and proof reading
Cristopher Yap

Graphic Design
Inês Veiga, inesveiga@gmail.com

Title for citation
CABANNES, Y. (ed.) (2017) *Another city is possible with Participatory budgeting*. Montréal/New York/London: Black Rose Books

Table of contents

ISSUE BRIEFS Cabannes, Y

RESOURCE FILES Cabannes, Y and Delgado, C

Presentation of the series and the book

Another city is possible with Participatory Budgeting

Brief introduction to the series Alternatives to the City as a Commodity

In cities and neighbourhoods throughout the world, citizens and communities are resisting, organizing themselves and generating alternatives to challenge an imposed urbanization model based solely on market rules that systematically generates social and economic exclusion. These alternatives mitigate the negative impacts of a crisis, sometimes referred to as "3F" (Food, Fuel and Finance).

Over the next years a series of books will be published as part of the collection **Alternatives to the city as a commodity.** They introduce some of these alternatives and their actors and also include written and visual resources for those who want to know more and become involved. These are far from exhaustive accounts of the alternative ways that people are building "other possible and liveable cities", realising utopian ideals envisioned through the World Social Forum. However, each one of the alternatives listed below corresponds, in our opinion, to the most promising ways to reclaim the "Right to the City":

- Participatory Budgeting
- Community Land Trusts (CLTS) and other forms of Collective and Communal forms of land Tenure
- Alternatives to forced evictions – staying in place
- Complementary and local currencies
- Urban and peri-urban Agriculture, from a food sovereignty perspective
- Housing and Employment co-operatives

Each one of these six topics plays a key role in an alternative urban production system, beyond simply market rules. And yet whilst each one of them is expanding remarkably in different parts of the world, their combination as a system is under-developed. This is due, in part, to the insufficient dialogue between leading actors. Therefore by documenting these experiences and connecting those who are behind them, this series will address a double challenge: the first is to link-up, put in perspective and potentially unify, these different initiatives, both globally and locally. The second is to shift scale and transformative capacity in order to generate a strong alternative to the production of housing and the city as a mere commodity. We are convinced a decisive step into shifting scale comes from linking up these alternatives.

Each one of these books offers a set of around 25 four-page briefings comprising: about 12 case studies; cross sectional analysis; synthesis; threads between the cases in order to go beyond localism; recommendations to scale up; existing and potential bridges between one issue and the five others in order to 'weave" the system (for instance how PB can and is being used to fund urban agriculture on a regular basis and strengthen food sovereignty); introductions to key players internationally and locally. Accessible basic references, introduction to key websites and a selected filmography complement each one of the files, that are at the same time standing alone and inter-connected. These briefings are written in the language used at least by some of the people where the experience is built: Spanish, Chinese, Portuguese, English or French.

The experiences briefly introduced are only the tip of the iceberg. They were selected from many examples according to five criteria:

[i] Radicalism in terms of deep and structural positive transformation of a given situation (an eviction, unemployment, etc.), and contribution to direct or at least participatory democracy, and citizen empowerment;

[ii] Availability and accessibility of information such as field notes, testimonies or grey literature;

[iii] Close contact with those who are or have been implementing the alternative, in order to complement and validate what is written;

[iv] Innovation: each case focuses on some innovative aspects more than on the whole story;

[v] Bridges, existing, planned or potential with the other five issues from the collection (key criteria).

These alternatives mirror the state of struggles and of utopias that turned reality and therefore permanently evolve. The whole project would lose any meaning if active and committed readers were not enriching it. You are therefore invited to share experiences worth documenting.

Using concise, organised and reflexive data, **Alternatives to the city as a commodity**, aims to contribute to the various Forums that will pave the way future World Social Forum that will gather thousands of people struggling for a better life. Despite its quite modest character, the collection posits a "counter-hegemonic" perspective towards the dominant discourse on the city and our urban future. These files will hopefully fuel international exchange, showcase innovation and highlight significant experience in the field of both Direct and Participatory Democracy.

Presentation of the book

This book consists of 24 chapters, or files organized into four sections: [1] The first one identifies the challenges, gives some keys of understanding and introduces the cases studied; [2] thirteen innovative PB experiences from a wide range of cities mirror the diversity of participatory budgeting processes world-wide; [3] The next three deal with cross-sectional issues, informed by the cases and; [4] Three resource briefs, introducing a basic bibliography, a selection of films, and a selection of accessible web sites complement the book and bring unique information on multiple experiences that could not be described or analyzed.

1. Background and challenges

The first three information briefs are analytical and conceptual. They familiarize the reader with some key issues:

- **The role of participatory budgeting** explains the book's inner logic and the specific contribution of participatory budgeting in "building another kind of city."

- **Basics on participatory budgeting:** includes definitions (i.e., what is participatory budgeting?); the concept's evolution since 1989; and proposes

three simple analytical tools that help differentiating one experience from another.
- **No blue print for participatory budgeting** puts in perspective the various experiences presented in the book and illustrate how diverse they are.

2. Case files

They cover cities of all size and all kinds: small towns and village, like Dondo in Mozambique; middle-size cities and regional capitals such as Belo Horizonte in Brazil, Rosario in Argentina, Seville in Spain, or Ilo in Peru; cities located at the periphery of large metropolitan areas, such as Guarulhos in São Paulo Metropolitan region or Cascais in metropolitan Lisbon and Global cities such as Paris. Some of these experiments take place at Metropolitan level for instance in Chengdu, China that counts over 15 million inhabitants. The book introduces the reader to experiments implemented at "infra-urban" levels—for example, in city wards, like *"Commune d'Arrondissement 6"* in Yaoundé, Cameroon or Chicago's 49th Ward. It also presents "supra-municipal" experiments, occurring, for instance, at regional level, such as in the high schools *(lycées)* of the Nord Pas de Calais Region in France.

These thirteen case studies also reflect considerable diversity in terms of the time span over which participatory budgeting has been used: eight of them have been in place for more than 10 years and up to 28 years as for Porto Alegre, the others range from 3 years as for Paris to 8 years, as in Seville or Chengdu. This diversity will hopefully shed light on how the volatility of these experiments can be reduced. Though the briefings are in narrative form and tell stories, they also offer some answers to practical questions, notably (1) where when, who, and what? ; (2) why?; (3) how?; (4) the experiment's relevance and broader interest; (5) what obstacles were faced and how where they overcome?

Finally, they illustrate the different "families" of participatory budgeting, as well as their combinations, which are often mixed up:
- Actor's based participatory budgeting for instance for women such as in Rosario or for the youth such as in La Serena in Chile,
- Thematic participatory budgeting, for example, related to housing, as in Belo Horizonte
- Spatially based or Territorial participatory budgets, which occur at neighborhood / district /city levels and are the most commonly found.

Snapshot on the thirteen Participatory Budgeting narratives from diverse regions in the world:

Chicago, 49th Ward, USA is a sub-municipal PB and a pioneering case in the USA with an effort to facilitate the participation of the excluded young people and African Americans.

Cascais, Portugal: information and communication technologies (voting by text messaging; governance and strong relations with the public; ties to Agenda 21; openness to innovation (for instance, local currencies); urban agriculture.

Belo Horizonte, Brazil is a paradigmatic thematic PB focused on Housing that allowed to build mutual aid multi-storey developments and collective property.

Guarulhos, São Paulo focuses on mass education and the need to transform citizens to transform cities.

Dondo, Mozambique is a unique example of PB as a driver of good governance.

La Serena, Chile highlights an innovative case of PB for primary and secondary school students.

Rosario, Argentina remains a reference for PB. This file use Rosario experience to illustrate an analytical grid that can be used to establish city PB profiles.

Ilo, an industrial port located south of Peru that decides 100 % of its capital budget through PB and set up a unique democratic governance model.

Seville, Spain, one of the most advanced European participatory budgeting experiences at a point in time, unfortunately interrupted in 2012.

Yaoundé, Ward 6, Cameroon, has reached, despite numerous obstacles, a way to democratization and improvement of living conditions in very poor local governments.

Nord Pas de Calais Region experiments conducted on a large scale in high schools and *lycées* of all kinds in one of the most deprived French Region.

Chengdu, Sichuan, China: Participatory budgeting as a way to reducing the urban – rural divide in China over 40,000 projects were decided upon by people and implemented in three years only.

Paris, France: the most recent of the experiences included in this book has expanded swiftly in only three years into a creative set of different PBs, at district and city levels, for schools and colleges and for lower income neighborhoods. The call for ideas and projects that kicks off the process has triggered citizen's imagination and their capacity to generate thousands of creative proposals to build another possible city and reclaim their "Right to the City".

3. Issue briefs

In order to go beyond these case studies and avoid falling into the trap of isolated experimentation, this section of the book explores key issues that are illustrated by the different cases:

- **Contribution of participatory budgeting to the democratization of governance at local level** that these various experiments have created and which represents one of the major contributions of participatory budgeting.
- **Continuity and discontinuity of participatory budgeting** processes deals with the conditions that are necessary to reduce the risks of interruption of experiences. It gives the voice to successful actors in the field that explain how they addressed this crucial issue.
- **Recommendations further radicalize PB** in order to fully release its potential as a powerful instrument to democratize radically democracy, that in its turn is probably one of the best way to build "another possible city' and alternatives to cities as a commodity.
- **The last text sheds light on some empirical connections between participatory budgeting and other issues dealt with in the collection,** ranging from urban agriculture, housing and employment cooperatives, or alternatives to evictions. Based on studies and the testimony of participants, it provides concrete information on the nature of these connections and how participatory budgeting has or has not contributed to strengthening them. It suggests as well recommendations for building bridges between PB and least connected themes like Community Land Trust or local currencies.

4. Resource files

The book's final part is for those who would like to go further, by deepening their knowledge through study but particularly by engaging in action:

- **A Bibliography of "Must-Reads"** that introduces a selection of 25 accessible and annotated sources.

- **A Selection of films** that introduces and comments 15 documentaries and movies in several languages on participatory budgeting covering the period between 2002 and 2017. It is complemented with 25 additional ones of interest available on Internet.

- **Forty web sites** on participatory budgeting in several work languages with the most important being described and commented upon.

The Urgent Need to Overcome Citizens' Distrust

Foreword

Anne Hidalgo, the Mayor of Paris

At a time when advancing transparency and citizen participation in public policy is urgently needed, it is both instructive and essential to recognise inspiring initiatives already being implemented.

In recent years, we have seen that the global economic crisis has fragmented the social cohesion and democratic consensus upon which our countries were built. A significant number of citizens despair, doubting the capacity of elected representatives to understand their expectations and to translate them into concrete action. Many are convinced that, whatever happens, their voice will not be listened to, nor taken into account. Hence, a notable rise of abstention, rendering illegitimate the very institutions that the citizens judge ineffective.

This is an extremely dangerous vicious circle for democracy – a vicious circle that we have the duty, the responsibility, and, moreover, the ability to break. We have to put an end to this sense of exclusion, to the enduring sense of pyramid-like decision making. There is an urgent need to overcome this phenomenon of mistrust in order to restore the confidence necessary for the functioning of our democracies.

The solution is well within our reach: it implies opening wide the gates of politics and inviting the involvement of our citizens within all the processes of reflection and decision making which concern them.

In Paris, we are pushing for the large scale incursion of all citizens into the democratic life of their city, and for their involvement at all levels of public policymaking. We have decided to devote substantial resources for this endeavour: the participatory budget that we have launched represents 5% of the total municipal investment budget, equalling 500 million euros between 2014 and 2020. This amount is the highest in the world for this type of initiative.

It is essential to us that all Parisians be able to vote – regardless of their age or nationality. This is because democracy is not a dead language, it must be spoken and used by all of us: every day and in all circumstances.

This is also why we have wished to create a participatory budget specifically dedicated for schools and colleges. In 2017, an amount of 10 million euros has been assigned to them, so that young Parisians can be stakeholders in their own educational destiny and live a concrete experience of citizenship from a very early age.

The participatory budget faces another major challenge: reconciling city government with a citizenry that feels *"invisible to the legal world of political decision making."* (Pierre Rosanvallon) This is the reason why, since 2016, we decided to reserve 30% of the total funds to be used for projects in working class neighbourhoods, making the participatory budget an additional tool for equality and social inclusion. Funding is also provided for the financing of associations that are working on initiatives in these neighbourhoods.

Fear Not Debate Nor Transparency

Naturally, undertaking such a project means accepting criticism, debate and conflict and proceeding in total transparency with citizens. So we must fear not debate – because it is in dialogue that we become aware of our differences and convergence – nor transparency – because it is in the eyes of the citizen that democracy flourishes.

Let's remind ourselves of the words of Christopher Lasch: *"What democracy requires is public debate, not information. Of course it needs information too, but the kind of information is needs can be generated only by vigorous popular debate."* My course of action is to discuss and debate everything. I am convinced that the confrontation of all perspectives is fruitful. Let's mobilize as broadly as possible, let's listen, let's discuss, let's compare ideas and we will see new horizons unfolding. Over the first years of my mandate, we have not made any decision unless it has passed the test of dialogue. I am confident that tomorrow's solutions will emerge through the sharing of ideas and the collaboration of public actors, companies, researchers, associations, and citizens.

The response of locally elected representatives to the crisis of confidence and conscience that is now undermining our democracy is not to fear the people nor stigmatise their choices: it is to show confidence by giving people more space to express themselves, more tools to learn, more power to truly influence decisions.

It is up to us to encourage direct democracy, which has its rightful place alongside elected bodies. Such a democracy corresponds to the definition which Jaures liked to give the Republic as "a great act of trust". Giving the citizens the keys to the budget is a show of faith that our societies so badly need today in order to come together and move forward.

The Role of Cities

In this context, I am convinced that cities have a special role to play. The twenty-first century is their century: cities now host more than half of the world's population. For several years, mayors have learned to work together, drawing inspiration from each other and constantly sharing experiences, good practices and common ambitions.

Besides, the Parisian participatory budget only came to life thanks to initiatives already undertaken abroad. It is because other cities such as Porto Alegre, Lisbon and New York had already experimented with this that we were able to go further by creating the largest participatory budget ever imagined.

Following Paris, even more cities such as Madrid, Milan and Stockholm followed suit and launched their own participatory budgets. Cities are at the forefront of democratic innovations and it is a fundamental and exciting mission that they lead together.

Let's Spread the Forces of Good

The Parisian experience has proved that when power is restored to citizens, the latter seize it. In 2016, for the third edition of the participatory budget, over 3,000 ideas were proposed and nearly 160,000 people voted to decide the future of their city. This figure is more than double that of the previous edition.

We are proud to have opened this new field of possibility in Paris. We will continue along this path with determination for we believe that it is the only way to turn mistrust into trust.

I can only hope that Yves Cabannes's formidable work convinces other cities to launch their own participatory budgets. Let us give the floor and give power to all the forces of the future, forces of peace. They are our greatest chance and our greatest hope.

Picture on the next page: City of Paris. Communication material on PB: *with participatory budgeting, you can notice change. Vote!*

AVEC LE BUDGET PARTICIPATIF,

LE CHANGEMENT

ÇA SE VOIT

PARIS BUDGET PARTICIPATIF

VOTEZ !

Du 16 septembre au 2 octobre 20h
Tous les lieux, toutes les infos sur
budgetparticipatif.paris

Part 1

BACKGROUND AND CHALLENGES

The Role of Participatory Budgeting and its specific contribution to building "another possible city"

The Role of Participatory budgeting and its specific contribution to building "another possible city"

Author
Cabannes, Yves
ycabanes@mac.com

Date
2014
Update 4/2017

Launching the series, **"Another City is possible! Alternatives to the city as a commodity"**, with a on Participatory Budgeting is no accident: our central argument in the series is that PB is the topic that connects best with other large struggles and experiments such as those happening in urban agriculture from a perspective of food sovereignty, Community Land Trusts and other collective and communal forms of tenure, Housing and Work cooperatives, local currencies, and resistance against evictions. All together, if united or interconnected, they seem the most promising avenues that lead to "another possible city" and that contribute to the realization of the "Right to the City". Before exploring briefly these connections and synergies occurring in some cities we would like to give a general overview of PB developments in the world and develop our argument along three lines.

The central argument for this book is that the most advanced Participatory Budgeting processes, including the various experiences described herein, do contribute to the struggle for the **Right to the City,** as theorized by Henri Lefebvre in a series of seminal books[1], published from 1968 to 1974. Participatory budgeting also contributes to reclaiming the central role of **deliberation for direct democracy and participatory democracy,** and finally to the

---

1 Series of H. Lefebvre books on city and urban related issues: Le droit à la ville, 1968; Du rural à l'urbain, 1970; La revolution urbaine, 1970; La pensée marxiste et la ville, 1972; Espace et politique second tome du droit à la ville, 1972; La production de l'espace, 1974.

transformation of parts of the city into **public urban commons**, which are essential for the Right to City ideals to flourish.

1. PB is here to stay! Introducing a quiet revolution

From nothing in 1989, to well over 3000 experiences in over 45 countries from all regions in the world by 2017. No one could have predicted such a success for Participatory Budgeting (PB), In a nutshell PB boils down to *"a mechanism or a process through which people make decisions on the destination of all or a portion of public resources available – in most cases at city level – or else are associated to the decision making process"*[2].

PB stands as one of the very few real democratic innovations over the last 30 years. Interestingly it took its first formal shape in the streets and the neighborhoods of Porto Alegre in the aftermath of a dark time of dictatorship in Brazil, and not in the air-conditioned offices of some international agencies, or in the minds of progressive and well-intentioned experts. In the past three decades, PB has been reinvented many times and has taken many different forms. Moreover, various innovative PB processes were designed locally with very limited contact, if any, with the original Brazilian processes. This is the case for instance for Ilo, Peru and Chengdu, China that are reported in this book. Despite huge obstacles, political and judicial opposition, failures, interruptions, and dropouts, nothing has been able to stop PB's swift expansion. The warnings and forecasts that I have heard over the past 20 years – "It is impossible in China"; "It is impossible in the USA"; and more recently, "It is impossible in Arab countries" – all proved wrong.

One of the critiques of PB has been that it debates and allocates very limited amounts of public resources. This might be true in some cases, and understandable in some contexts where local authorities, for example in some African countries or Haiti, have a meager budget of less than US $5 per habitant per year. But in other contexts this amount can be 1000 times higher. However, as suggested by the stories told here, the financial and budgetary dimensions are only one aspect of PB. PB's virtues, such

---

2 Early definition of PB coined by Uribatam de Souza in 1989, while engaged in the first PB experiment in Porto Alegre, Brazil.

as reclaiming the Right to the City and changing peoples' everyday lives, go much beyond money and budget. This being said, the sums at stake globally and in some cities are far from being insignificant. A participatory budgeting review across 20 cities from different regions that examined over 20,000 projects found that over US $2 billion had been spent in three years through PB processes[3]. Chengdu alone, referred to in chapter 15, had invested over US $1.2 billion between 2009 and 2016 in over 50 000 projects. Paris (see chapter 16) earmarked €500 million for PB for 2014-2016, and Madrid announced €100 million for its 2016 PB cycle.

Large amounts of money are not only allocated through PB in large cities, as demonstrated by the cases of São Bernardo do Campo, a rich municipality of 700 000+ inhabitants located in São Paulo Metropolitan Region, Brazil [over US $180 million in 2011 and 2012], and Ilo, a small coastal city south Peru of less than 70 000 inhabitants, that allocates 100% of its budget through PB. In Ilo, as a result US $13.1 million was debated in 2012 and the experience has now lasted for 19 years (see chapter 11). The resources debated through Ilo PB reached the remarkable figure of US $208 per inhabitant per year. Claiming that PB is financially insignificant is simply wrong.

One can wonder then why PB is still largely ignored by local government organizations, such as United Cities and Local Governments [UCLG], with a notable exception for its African chapter that promotes PB and tries to increase its legitimacy. After a couple of years of interest and support, UN-Habitat, the United Nations agency for cities lost interest in PB and the New Urban Agenda, endorsed by most governments world wide at Habitat III in October 2016, does not make any explicit reference to what has being widely practiced since before Habitat II in 1996. Understanding the omission from international agendas remains an open issue. At the same time, it shows how global organizations face the risk of becoming obsolete, simply because they are not able to respond societal changes and peoples' evolving aspirations. As a result, and in front of a collective incapacity to grasp the multiplicity of PB processes in the world, the present book shows simply the tip of an iceberg and remains a testimony of what various

---

3   Cabannes Y, Contribution of Participatory Budgeting to provision of basic services in cities, Environment & Urbanization, 2015 International Institute for Environment and Development (IIED). Vol 27(1): 257–284

authors and filmmakers call **a silent or a quiet revolution** (see for instance Santadreu, 2007[4], or the documentary film, a quiet revolution, directed by P. Stoeber, 2014[5]).

2. Capitals and global cities, new stars in the PB sky

PB experiments are expanding in all directions and regions, and in cities of all kinds, from villages to megacities. Global crises and people's aspirations and struggles have kept cities as lively laboratories for change. Most PB processes still occur at municipal- and/or district-level, and much less at regional- or provincial-level. The experience that began in 2017 in Portugal, of a national PB, that will debate the symbolic value of €3 million needs to be mentioned here as breaking new ground.

Capitals cities need a special mention for the innovative and radical processes that they have fostered in recent years. Capital cities have, from 1989, experimented with PB in different ways and at different scales. Among the most well known are Montevideo, Bogota, Federal District of Mexico or Yaoundé, which stand as illustrative and innovative examples. In the early 2000's São Paulo became the first city of 10 million inhabitants to introduce PB at a significant scale. It was the first time that a large, global city was putting huge sums of money, over US $100 million per year, under discussion through PB.

What is new and exciting is that over the last few years, more and more capital and global cities are engaging in more radical PB processes, despite their complexities and in spite of the limits of existing systems: New York, Paris, Madrid, Delhi, Taipei or Seoul are interesting examples. This emergence results from bottom up, or top down initiatives or a combination of both. They are breaking new ground and each one of them brings cutting edge ways to build progressive cities; more democratic and more humane.

On the one hand civil society organizations, such as PB Project in **New York** or *Citizen Action Network* in Seoul, are spearheading PB "from below" and reflect a new and more radical way to look at democracy. New York [8.5 million+ inhabitants in 2015] started PB in 2012 in 4 wards that allocated over US $5 million, along the model tested in Chicago's 49th Ward (see chapter 4). In an unpublished report, PB Project highlights that most wards in NYC have gradually engaged in PB [31 in 2016] representing in the range of US $35 million in 2016. Interestingly none of them had dropped out and remained active since their start [PBP USA, staff report September 2016, unpublished].

On the other hand, District and City Mayors, coming from the political left and/or from Civic and Rights-based movements are committing themselves to PB and participatory processes, spearheading movements and changes that are worth understanding:

Bogotá, 8 million+ inhabitants in 2017, went through a radical PB change, during the mandate of Mayor Gustavo Petro. Over his 2012-2015 mandate the Program, *Participate and Decide,* part of the city-wide strategy, *Bogota Humana,* earmarked US $74.4 million for PB through the 20 districts of the capital. PB became a way to engage with the youth, for peace making and to end urban violence. A remarkable book[6], tells the story of how PB can change youth life and support positive actions in violent and complex neighborhoods. Mayor Petro comes from the radical left; at a time part of Guerrilla movement M19 and currently part of the *Movimiento progresista.*

In **Seoul,** another newcomer in PB in capital cities, the process is not only spearheaded by radical grassroots and civil society organizations such as National PB network, Citizen Action Network, and the Centre for Good Budget, but at the same time by the Mayor himself, Park Won-soon; Park trained as a lawyer and with a long standing commitment as a human rights activist.

Madrid is another illustrative and excellent case of a highly committed and radical Mayor, Manuela Carmena, who brought her authority and capacity to implement PB at quite a significant scale. With a long history in the Spanish Communist Party, she was elected as a "Citizens' Candidate of Peoples Unity", called *Ahora Madrid* [Madrid Now]. The PB process started in September 2015 as a web platform <decide.madrid.es>, giving the opportunity to any citizen over 16 years old to propose and vote for projects.

---

6   See: Somos la generación de de la paz, experiencias de participación juvenil y presupuesto participativo en Bogota, 200 pages, 2016.

In 2016, the process was consolidated with €100 million, earmarked for the city and its districts. As in Paris, solidarity with the homeless and the excluded, (discussed later in the book), became a priority, with resources amounting to €700 000. These original examples of projects, not frequent in PB processes, illustrate our hypothesis of PB as a facilitator of "Other possible cities". The role and profiles of the Mayors in all cities mentioned is decisive for radicalizing PB, and beyond the tendency to use it as a way of optimizing financial resources or as a tool for good governance. Three motivations for PB are currently identifiable: one that aims, explicitly or implicitly to radicalize democracy and give more power to people. It is the one referred to here and the most conducive to realizing the Right to the City, and lead to alternatives to the city as a commodity. The second motivation, more technocratic, intends to improve relations between local governments and citizens, and aims at improving governance. The third is essentially managerial and aims at rationalizing financial public resources in a time of supposedly doomed austerity. Tensions between these three motivations for PB are discussed in file 3.

3. PB as a mechanism to reclaim the Right to the City

Our take on the Right to the City goes back to Henry Lefebvre's seminal definition, coined in 1968: *The Right to the City manifests itself as a superior form of rights: right to freedom, right to individualization in socialization, to habitat and to inhabit. The right to the oeuvre , to participation, and appropriation [clearly distinct from the right to property], are implied in the right to the city*[7]. An exploration of the narratives on PB processes permits us to illustrate the multiple ways radical PB experiences are conducive to reclaiming this superior form of Rights. The approach here is quite different and goes way beyond those that work on rights in the city that are usually referring to a bundle of rights that would be contained in the Right to The City. Two main Charters have been formulated so far: the **Global Charter for Human Rights in the City** formulated by local governments belonging to United Cities and Local Governments [UCLG] Commission

---

7 « Le droit à la ville se manifeste comme forme supérieure des droits: droit à la liberté, à l'individualisation dans la socialisation, à l'habitat et à l'habiter. Le droit à l'œuvre (a l'activité participante] et le droit à l'appropriation (bien distinct du droit à la propriété) s'impliquent dans le droit à la ville »

on Social Inclusion, Participatory Democracy and Human Rights. The second entitled, **Global Charter on the Right to the City**, results from a long process spearheaded by a collective of NGOs, part of the Habitat International Coalition [HIC]. These charters propose a set of individual and collective bundle of rights in the city. In other words, the Right to the City encompasses rights in the city, but cannot be limited to them.

A second observation is that the Right to the City as described by Lefebvre deals with the City as a whole, leaving un-described what citizens and movements are struggling for, the Right to a Place, to live in peace in dignity. When communities are facing evictions to stay in place, they struggle for their own neighborhood with all its life, culture, art and livelihoods, but not for a City as such. What most radical PBs are reclaiming is the Right to the City as a superior form of Rights, and at various urban scales: neighborhoods, districts and the city as a whole. This is the case in Paris, Madrid and Belo Horizonte, where part of the PB resources are earmarked for the districts and other parts for projects at the city-scale. Another way to realize this right at the scale of the neighborhood and the City as a whole, is to earmark part of the PB resources for specific sectors [mobility, environment, social economy, etc.] at the city-level, and another part for projects at neighborhood and district level (see file 3 for further explanation).

Generating public commons and Ágoras

A common thread across hundreds of PB experiences and projects are those related to the development, improvement and rehabilitation of parks, squares, plazas, or idle and left over parcels of land, mostly in low income settlements. Again, and quite in line with Lefebvre's ideas, citizen's proposals reduce the privatization of public spaces, and essentially increase their use value. A Project in Yaoundé stands as an excellent illustration of this tendency. Other projects contained in this book [Belo Horizonte, Chicago, Guarulhos or La Serena could have been taken as well.]

In Yaoundé Commune 4, Nkolo District, people prioritized a public fountain at the district-level that serves now over 50 000 people.. Rapidly the site changed from a muddy and hardly accessible ground water well into an immaculate collective water point in quite a deprived and poor district (see picture). At the same time, the space became a meeting square for the elderly ensuring the good use of the water by the kids and youth in charge of filling in buckets for their homes, a stand for women, and sometimes men, to wash and dry clothes in the open, and place for kids to play. It offers today a multi-functional area where different generations can interact, quite opposite to the tendency to mono-functional areas of the few public spaces in "modern" Yaoundé. The quality of the maintenance of the area by people from the district echoes the conclusions from the research on appropriation of urban spaces produced through PB, presented further ahead. It appears that appropriation, in the same sense as Lefebvre, is a key ingredient to keep PB projects much better maintained than others built by the state without citizen participation.

Reclaiming land use instead of privatization and land ownership

Probably one of the most significant ways PB projects do contribute to building the Right to the City is through projects that challenge the tendencies existing in most cities to commodify urban land, and to reduce its use to a limited number of people. Two examples are illustrative. In Buffalo, USA, PB started in 2016 (see picture) on a modest scale from a budgetary view point but voted to support local farmers markets on high streets and another central avenues. In doing so, Buffalo citizens are reclaiming the multi-use of the streets, in tune with Lefebvre claim to reclaim the multi-use of public spaces, for the benefit of all, and the improvement of everyday life. In Seville, urban farmers from different low-income neighborhoods and from poor high rise tenements development areas mobilized to get quite significant support from PB to improve the farming parks and the allotments they reclaimed. Their request was to improve as well drainage and irrigation systems. At no point in time, was property part of the proposals: people were essentially interested in the appropriation of large spaces that became for some of them multi-functional spaces opened to the city for cultural, leisure, training and farming activities.

Aesthetics and art

In a rare video interview dating from 1972, Lefebvre explains how functionalist architects and planners, starting with Le Corbusier himself, as well as the *Bahaus* architects, have left aside essential functions that are needed to make cities socially habitable: aesthetics is one of them, the ludic dimension another key one. However when they are taken into account by functionalists, symbols and symbolic values are reduced to commercial values.

PB projects such as vertical gardens in Paris, or multi-storey blind façades and dark spaces under bridges painted by graffiti artists in Paris or Chicago (see pictures in respective chapters] are ways to reclaim the central value of *inhabiting* [understood as non-segregated urban spaces where lively social life can happen).

Connecting the dots: from the Right to Place, to the Right to the City

Mobility projects highly ranked in PB processes in Seville, Spain and Guarulhos, Brazil (see files). While these experiences were technically quite different, they share similar logics in terms of reclaiming the Right to the City. Seville citizens from different neighborhoods voted massively for a citywide bike lane. Its design was far from most bike lanes projects that are usually in central areas, which connect housing to districts of consumption such as restaurant and cafés, museums or heritage monuments. In the case of Seville the design, decided along with citizens, connects places socially, economically and culturally meaningful for people, to allow them to use the city more freely and reduce their traveling costs. Practically Seville bike lanes connect low-income settlements, between themselves and with places of work or universities and schools. The impact on the transport system was remarkable and testified by the increase of users. It helped re-unify the fragmented city, largely criticized by Lefebvre. The new bus terminal and improvement of the public system in Guarulhos, a one-million+ municipality in São Paulo Metropolitan Region], obeys to the same logic of increasing the possibility for people from low income settlements to better access and use their city as a whole.

Exploring appropriation of space produced through PB

A pioneering research (Murta, 2006) explored the appropriation of urban space, in the very sense of Lebebvre, produced as a result of the PB process

---

8 Sant' Anna Murta, Anamaria, "Projeção inversa": da prática do orçamento participativo à apropriação do espaço urbano, Dissertação apresentada ao Curso de Pós-Graduação em Ciências Sociais da Pontifícia Universidade Católica de Minas Gerais, 2006, p. 230

in Belo Horizonte, Brazil from 1994, when it started, to 2004[8]. Four variables were used for this exploration:
- Conservation / Maintenance of the urban space produced through the PB process,
- Symbolic and affective value of the work: care for public and private buildings,
- Use of the space built through the PB process and,
- Residents remaining in the neighbourhood despite the rise of land value (Sant' Anna Murta, op cit).

The research concludes that when citizen are able to make decisions about the use of public resources, they tend to develop new forms of relationship with the public administration and to appropriate the spaces built in a participatory way. Such a conclusion highlights that the first phase of PB that ends with the selection of a particular project is not enough for the appropriation of space. It is determined as well by citizens' participation in what is called in this book the second cycle of PB that stretches from the budgetary decision to the actual implementation of a particular project. Participation in design, or through the bidding process, and to select enterprises or in the co-implementation of a project, as developed in Belo Horizonte (see files 6.1 and 6.2) were essential to explain why people stayed in the neighbourhoods and in the houses built through PB, despite an increase of local land taxes, increase in rental values, and a growing interest of real estate enterprises. Ownership of PB projects by people greatly explains high levels of appropriation of spaces.

4. An exploration of connections between PB and other alternatives to build "other possible cities".

A comparative advantage of participatory budgeting in relation to other alternatives comes from its scale and territorial anchoring. It can cover entire cities or metropolis and offer fruitful opportunities to foster experiments and innovations such as cooperatives, urban agriculture, or Community Land Trusts that have smaller spatial scales, and that can be funded through participatory budgeting. This book explores several of these bridges but it is a far from an exhaustive account of all the potential ones.

Participatory budgeting and urban agriculture from a food sovereignty perspective

Under pressure from residents, neighborhood associations, and urban farmer groups, some cities have incorporated urban agriculture projects as eligible participatory budgeting projects. Porto Alegre was probably one of the first cases when peach growers requested funding through participatory budgeting to market their fruit directly during the high production season, when prices plummet and producers have to sell their fruit at any cheap price, before the fruit gets rotten. Thanks to participatory budgeting an annual producers' fair takes place in the center of the city, close to the main market. As a result, a direct marketing link connected local producers and urban consumers. This is far from being a marginal example as Porto Alegre, in addition to being the capital of one of Brazil's most developed States, is also the fourth largest peach producer in the highly agricultural state of Rio Grande do Sul. This annual fair, which was made possible for several years by participatory budgeting, has become a regular event. Now, few of its inhabitants even remember the launching of this initiative some twenty years ago.

Similarly, the city of Rosario, following the crisis that shook Argentina in the early 2000s, agreed to finance urban agriculture projects, yielding to pressure from old *piqueteros* and groups of urban agriculture producers that had been formed to deal with an unprecedented crisis. In a completely different context, as a result of the pioneering experiment in participatory budgeting in Chicago's 49th Ward, residents voted to make the community garden one of their priorities. The garden has been very productive. All of these cases will be discussed in this book.

Interestingly all three winning projects for the first cycle of Participatory Budgeting [2016] in Buffalo relate to food. Over 300 residents, still a modest number for an American city approaching one million inhabitants, came out to vote at 8 different locations and decided that the 150 000 dollars available should be spent on: a farmer's market on Main Street; community Kitchen upgrades for a community center; and support for a Healthy Cooking Campaign. This example, however small it might appear, once again illustrates the multiple bridges between PB and other alternatives that happen in an increasing number of cities and towns.

Participatory budgeting, housing and employment cooperatives

Some significant experiments illustrate the various connections established on the ground between participatory budgeting and cooperative initiatives. Cities such as Porto Alegre or Belo Horizonte in Brazil are clear examples. In Belo Horizonte (see narrative in the book) for instance a dozen of self managed developments benefiting thousands of homeless people were built through mutual aid and funded through PB. They resulted from lobby and struggle from housing movements and organized groups of homeless.

Participatory budgeting and Community Land Trusts

While relations between PB and CLTs are not as direct as those with urban agriculture and housing cooperatives, it is worth noting that in cities like Chicago, participatory budgeting has developed in parallel with Community land Trusts. Though they are not yet connected, their respective promoters and champions recently expressed the mutual benefit that would result from connecting these initiatives, as they are based on *"shared ethical values primarily community ownership of the process."*[9]

Participatory budgeting, local and complementary currencies

A number of cities that practice participatory budgeting started to show interest in establishing closer connections between these two alternatives. The central idea proposed here is that participatory budget projects should not be funded in national currencies as they are today, but through local currencies that would be generated locally by local governments and by communities. The national currency earmarked for PB would then act as a reserve currency, which could guarantee local currencies. In a city like Várzea Paulista, in the state of São Paulo in Brazil, participatory budgeting and local currencies are promoted by the same groups—some in the community, some in the city government—without any connections being made between them so far. It seems highly likely that such connections will be established in the near future and will generate a much higher impact towards the transformation of the city.

---

9 Interview by author with Executive Director, Community Partners for Affordable Housing, Highland Park, Illinois, May 2013.

Participatory budgeting and alternatives to forced evictions

Most participatory budgets are primarily aimed at financing basic services, mainly at neighborhood level. However, a small number of initiatives such as the Housing Participatory Budgeting from Belo Horizonte, in Brazil have generated mutual aid housing opportunities for the homeless.

In Chengdu, the capital of Chinese Sichuan Province, PB is closely tied to the land reform of property law, thus allowing, for example, thousands of peasants in suburban Chengdu not only to avoid being evicted from their lands (contrary to many of their compatriots), but to elaborate projects that increased their income.

5. Participatory budgeting contributes to local development and to reclaiming urban commons

First, participatory budgets are financed primarily through endogenous resources primarily the municipal budget and therefore are deeply rooted in local realities. They are at the heart of development based on local capacities and resources. However, cities occasionally mobilize additional resources from central governments to finance or co-finance specific requirements of a participatory budget (see narrative on Guarulhos, Brazil). Furthermore, African cities that practice participatory budgeting have been able to significantly channel international aid to supplement their meager public budget. This is the case of the city of Dondo in Mozambique and of Yaoundé Commune 6 in Cameroun presented in the book.

PB as "commoning"

Throughout the vast literature that refers to Commons and intends to conceptualize it, Massimo de Angelis [An Achitektur, 2010] highlights that *"conceptualizing the commons involves three things at the same time. First, all commons involve some sort of common pool of resources, understood as non-commodified means of fulfilling peoples needs. Second, the commons are necessarily created and sustained by communities—this of course is a very problematic term and topic, but nonetheless we have to think*

---

10 Journal #17 - June 2010. An Architektur. On the Commons: A Public Interview with Massimo De Angelis and Stavros Stavrides

30

about it. [...] In addition to these two elements—the pool of resources and the set of communities—the third and most important element in terms of conceptualizing the commons is the verb "to common"—the social process that creates and reproduces the commons[10]. Our assumption is that participatory budgeting, at least in the most advanced cases (see file 17), are precisely processes of commoning in the very sense of de Angelis. A unique aspect to highlight is that PB creates urban commons in a relatively short period of time, usually one or two years, that correspond to the time to implement projects.

PB can generate public commons, quite different from community commons

The debate introduced by Stavros Stavridres [An Achitektur, op.cit] between commons and public is particularly interesting as it helps in identifying the added value of PB in relation to cities as commons. In his own words: *"First, I would like to bring to the discussion a comparison between the concept of the commons based on the idea of a community and the concept of the public. The community refers to an entity, mainly to a homogeneous group of people, whereas the idea of the public puts an emphasis on the relation between different communities. The public realm can be considered as the actual or virtual space where strangers and different people or groups with diverging forms of life can meet."*[11] A PB process, with its numerous assemblies, fora, councils at different scales in a particular city, is precisely this "virtual place" where different people can meet and debate. Various forms of PB, and not necessarily those that are basically on line processes, or limited to fragmented communities, are generating public *commons*, and avoid the trap of maintaining the commons based on the idea of fragmented communities.

To the question: How can these relations with those "others" be regulated? S. Stavridres highlights [An Achitektur, op.cit]: *"For me, this aspect of negotiation and contest is crucial, and the ambiguous project of emancipation has to do with regulating relationships between differences rather than affirming commonalities based on similarities".* Once again, most PB,

---

11 Journal #17 - June 2010. An Architektur. On the Commons: A Public Interview with Massimo De Angelis and Stavros Stavrides

through the space they offer for debates and deliberation between different actors contribute to regulate relationships between different citizens and different communities. They answer rather well to *"the need to "to find ways of giving room to negotiate the differences,"* stressed by Stravidres to generate public commons.

PB as a space of negotiating differences through deliberation

Restating deliberation as a crucial value of <u>direct and participatory democracy</u>

One of the emerging conclusions substantiated by the experiences presented here and existing literature on PB and deliberative democracy, is that one of PBs added value is to open up spaces and to give room for people to debate and discuss about the projects they want for their city. This deliberative quality of PBs, vary greatly from one city to the other and clearly emerges as an attribute of the most radical ones.

Anne Hidalgo, Mayor of Paris, in the foreword to this book, stresses not only the importance of debate and deliberation in the present context of PB but as a political position for her government: *"My course of action is to discuss and debate everything. I am convinced that the confrontation of all perspectives is fruitful. Let's mobilize as broadly as possible, let's listen, let's discuss, let's compare ideas and we will see new horizons unfolding".*

Such "new horizons" are quite in tune with the title of the book, *"Another city is possible with PB"*; they are the tens of thousands of creative projects resulting from the thousands of hours of deliberation and debates. One of the virtues of PB, in most cities described here, is that it gave people a voice. More importantly, it gave in many cases voice to the usually voiceless and most vulnerable, and power to those that are usually powerless. La Serena, Chile, and Rosario, Argentina referred to in the book printed vote bulletins and projects description in Braille language to include social groups usually excluded from citizens participation processes. In doing so, PB not only inverts social and political priorities, as referred to in Porto Alegre, in its early days, in some cities PB quite actively includes vulnerable groups as part of the process and the debates.

Deliberation, right to dissent and accept "dissensus"

Whilst consensus is commonly used in political sciences and participatory processes, *dissensus* is virtually not in use. The origin of this world of late Middle English origin, from c.1150 to c.1470, comes from the Latin dissentire, *"differ in sentiment"*. Today, as a noun or a verb, dissent refers to *"the holding or expression of opinions at variance with those commonly or officially held"* [Merriam Webster dictionary]. Interestingly, the same dictionary gives the following one sentence illustrative example: *"a democracy relies on dissensus as much as on consensus"*.

Our claim here, quite in line with Stravidres' argument is that because of the multiple channels and spaces that PB opens for dissenting voices to be heard, contributes powerfully to reclaiming deliberation as a central value for democracy and for shifting from community to public commons.

The challenge of knowledge production and knowledge management: Knowledge as a commons

Most of the experiences of PB implemented over nearly three decades have been lost, as they were barely documented, if at all. This holds true not only for small and intermediate cities or villages far from universities, research centers or NGOs, but for some capital cities just the same. For instance, most information and lessons on the PB process launched in Asunción, capital of Paraguay, are lost. The election of ex Catholic bishop Fernando Lugo as President in 2008 marked a turning point in Paraguayan Politics, which for decades was characterized by dictatorship and non-participatory governance. Soon after his election, quite an original PB process was launched in the capital city that unfortunately was stopped after 2012 when he was destitute through what appeared as a *coup d'état* and a violation of constitutional rights. This is only one example from thousands.

According to our estimates, solid information in different languages exists on around 200 PB experiences out of the 3000+ that exist today or that have flourished and disappeared. Most of the existing literature consists basically of institutional documentation produced by local governments or by NGOs that were involved in the process, which tends to disappear through time or when the experience ends. Chapter 17 on continuity and discontinuity of PB processes addresses this issue. Another level of information, much more succinct, but quite important to build collective memory on PB and extract lessons, comes from national evaluations such as the ones indicated in the file 18 on Germany, Argentina, Brazil, Indonesia, to name a few. In total they refer to a couple of hundred PB experiments, but are still far from covering the universe of PBs.

In summary the production of knowledge on PB experiences, primarily on the least accessible ones remains a challenge. Comparing these experiences, extracting lessons that are socially and politically useful for expanding the movement, and that exemplify PB values is another major challenge. Reclaiming knowledge as a common good is a critical precondition of the realization of the Right to the City on a major scale. In response to the expansion of PB world wide, it seems that knowledge produced through universities and research centers will remain a luxury for the years to come. If one considers that most applied research, including on PB, ends up solely in publications to serve primarily university purposes or the career interests of researchers with very little feed back to actors involved in the field. One can doubt that knowledge will be transformative and will help to scale the expansion of PB through out. There is a need to rethink the way to document these experiences and have them easily accessible and highly visible. *Social production of knowledge,* called sometimes co-production of knowledge, as it can involve researchers or academics on the one hand and citizens and civil servants on the other, might be a way to keep the pace with such huge transformations occurring in the field. The present book was developed in close relationship with actors involved in PB in their cities, which clearly shows that it is possible.

Basics tools for navigating the world of Participatory Budgeting

PARTICIPATORY BUDGETING
FILE
2
BACKGROUND/CHALLENGES

Basics tools for navigating the world of Participatory Budgeting

Author
Cabannes, Yves
ycabanes@mac.com

Date
2014
Update 4/2017

Defining "participatory budgeting"[1]

There is no single definition of Participatory budgeting; it is a concept and practice that varies significantly from one context to another. This book and the PB experiences related in it attempt to give an account of this diversity. Nonetheless, in a very general way, participatory budgeting is "*a mechanism or a process through which people make decisions on the destination of all or a portion of the public resources available or else are associated to the decision-making process.*"

Ubiratan de Souza, one of the pioneers of participatory budgeting in Porto Alegre Brazil, suggests a more accurate and theoretical definition that can be applied to the majority of cases in Brazil and beyond:

"*Participatory budgeting is a direct democracy process that is voluntary and universal through which people can debate and decide on budgets and public policies. Instead of being limited to electing those to occupy the executive and legislative branches of government, citizen participation also takes shape by making decisions on priority areas for spending and on how government management should be controlled. Citizens stop being the kingmakers in traditional politics and become permanent protagonists of public*

---

1 The first part of this file is adapted from our manual "72 Frequently Asked Questions on Participatory Budgeting" for UN-Habitat (Cabannes, 2004). The manual is available in seven languages. www.unhabitat.org/pmss/searchResults.aspx?sort=relevance&page=search&searchField=title&searchstring=72&x=21&y=5

administration. PB links direct democracy to representative democracy, an asset to be preserved and valued".

And so we should understand PB as a form of Participatory Democracy. In other words, it is made up of various components of direct and semi-direct democracy and representative democracy. The varying combinations of these different components make each PB experience unique.

A 25+ year old innovation that emerged in Brazil

Participatory budgeting emerged in 1989 in a limited number of cities in Brazil, such as Porto Alegre, although there were a few very limited experiences prior to that date. Beyond Brazil, in Montevideo, Uruguay, for example, people have been invited to give suggestions on how city resources should be used within the context of the five-year plan since 1990.

A steady PB expansion, phase by phase, since 1990

Four major phases of expansion can be identified. The first (1989-1997) was characterised by PB experiences in a small number of cities. The second (1997-2000) was marked by consolidation of the process in Brazil; during this phase, more than 130 cities adopted participatory budgeting. In the third phase that began at the turn of the twenty-first century PB spread beyond Brazil to other countries in Latin America. Highly significantly, in countries such as Peru and the Dominican Republic, PB was eventually adopted in all local governments. It spread gradually to Africa, Europe, and more recently, to Asia and the Arab world. From the middle of the first decade of the twenty-first century (2005-2017), a fourth phase of international consolidation can be identified, with national and international 'networks' of cities and stakeholders actively involved in participatory budgeting. These networks consolidated discussion and enabled PB experiences to be more visible. They were, in essence, lobbies and sounding boards that became increasingly powerful and influential on the international stage. In many cities and districts, nonetheless, PB processes remain weak and depend on the self-mobilisation of citizen associations' and ever-changing political will. In 2017, approximately 2500 cities and regions used participatory budgeting in many different forms, most of them still at an experimental stage. This explains (and indeed this is an advantage) why there is no single PB 'recipe' or model. There are PB processes that reflect local conditions and socio-political context that can variously enable or impede grassroots and public institutions.

In what type of cities has participatory budgeting been implemented?
Participatory budgeting is practiced in villages, cities and even regions of all shapes and sizes: from rural villages with a few hundred inhabitants; medium-sized cities with fewer than 100,000 inhabitants; districts like Yaoundé 6, or cities with around one million inhabitants such as Rosario, Argentina; to very large cities with more than 17 million people like Chengdu, China. Over the last years, a growing number of global cities an country capitals such as Paris, presented in this book, New York City, Madrid, Taipei, Seoul or Delhi are implementing successfully, on a significant scale various forms of quite radical and innovative participatory budgeting processes.

It is practiced in rural and semi-rural areas as well as in completely urbanised cities such as Belo Horizonte, presented in this book and in neighbourhoods on the outskirts of cities, such as Guarulhos in the metropolitan region of the city of São Paulo, Brazil. Participatory budgeting is used in cities with very limited public resources, such as the majority of Sub-Saharan African cities whose annual budget per inhabitant is less that US $3, as well as in European or Brazilian cities with public resources that are five hundred to one thousand times greater.

Three tools for understanding and differentiating very different PB experiences
We are proposing three tools for distinguishing specific types of PB from the plethora of PB experiences that have emerged and are still in operation.

1. Territorial, Thematic and Actor-based Participatory Budgeting
The vast majority of participatory budgeting mechanisms are *territorial*, i.e. they are conducted at the neighbourhood, district, communal and city levels. They embrace all areas over which the city is responsible if the budget is controlled at the city level, and, in theory, are designed to engage and benefit all inhabitants, even if all of them are not involved to the same extent or at all.

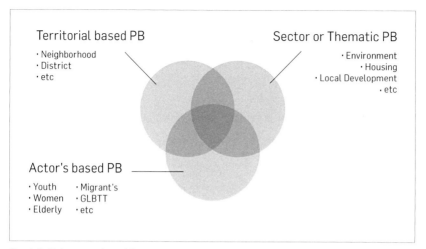

Graph 1: Main types of participatory budgeting

A second type of participatory budgeting is related to processes that debate, at city level, resources to be allocated to specific sectors such as education, basic services, employment, housing, transport, etc; this is *Thematic PB*. The Participatory Budgeting for Housing process in Belo Horizonte, Brazil, presented in this book, is a good example of this type of PB. The themes selected can change from year to year and reflect the changing city priorities and prerogatives. If city-level authorities are not responsible for education, the chances are that there will be no participatory budgeting for education.

A third type, unfortunately much less frequent, can be referred to as actor-based participatory budgeting which allocate specific resources for specific vulnerable groups: the elderly, indigenous groups, the African-Brazilian population in cities in Brazil, Lesbian-Gay-Bisexual-Transgender (LGBT) groups, immigrants or the homeless. Actor- based participatory budgeting comes generally with participatory methods and mechanisms that facilitate and embolden their involvement. In the present book, various actor-based PB will be introduced. For example in the case of participatory budgeting for children and young people that will be addressed by the case of La Serena, Chile (file 9), and participatory budgeting for women in Rosario, Argentina. Another example, participatory budgeting for secondary schools in the Nord-Pas-de-Calais Region, also presented, is particularly pioneering because it is a regional rather than a city level process.

Graph 1 outlines these three basic types of PB and mixed systems that combined them. All of the cases presented in this book are shown on the graph with additional notes.

2. Multi-variable analysis table, made up of 18 variables for creating participatory budgeting profiles

In an attempt to navigate the extremely diverse world of participatory budgeting, we propose a multi-criteria analysis table that has been tested and used in several cases since 2004[2], enabling them to be put into perspective. This table (see Graph 2) is comprised of columns with 18 variables, organised into four broad categories: (i) budgetary and fiscal; (ii) form/nature of participation, referring both to citizen participation and government participation; (iii) normative/institutional and legal and (iv) physical or spatial[3]. Each of these categories allow political dimensions and governance to be examined. The headings across the top of the table correspond to columns for minimal arrangement, intermediate arrangement and maximum arrangement. For example, for Variable 6, 'addressing oversight and control of projects decided on in the PB process', there is minimal arrangement when the process is conducted by the Office of the Mayor; arrangement is deemed intermediate if the process is carried out by non- specific/general committees (district associations) that include this task in their activities, and there is maximum arrangement if specific committees, such as Participatory Budgeting Councils, are elected during the PB process and given a genuine mandate.

It is then possible to gradually design a specific city profile, having under-stood that every year, the variables may change. Each of the variables is like a measurement tool that can pick up minor or major variations in the PB process. This grid works like a scoreboard and a strategic tool for citizens, city employees and locally elected representatives, to understand where they are, where they want to go and where they can go. It is, therefore, a

---

2 Cabannes for UN-Habitat (UN-Habitat, 2003: 20-21), available in English and Spanish. See also PMVP, Multi-variable Method for establishing PB city profiles. Available in Portuguese and English, to be published in 2014, Belo Horizonte.
3 An adapted version of this table was developed and tested during an evaluation workshop in Cameroon in 2011 and the category "employment and wealth creation" was added as a fifth category.

DIMENSIONS	VARIABLES	MINIMAL ARRANGEMENT	INTERMEDIATE ARRANGEMENT	MAXIMUM ARRANGEMENT
I PARTICIPATORY (citizens)	1. Forms of participation	Community-based representative democracy	Community-based representative democracy open to different types of associations	Direct democracy, universal participation
	2. Instance of final budget approval	Executive (partial consultation)	Council (consultative)	The population (deliberation and legislative approval)
	3. What body makes budgetary priority decisions?	None	Existing social or political structure Government and citizens (mixed)	Specific commissions with elected council members and a citizen majority
	4. Community participation or citizen participation	Neighborhood level	City-wide level, through thematic contributions	Neighborhood, regional, and city-wide level
	5. Degree of participation of the excluded	Thematic and neighborhood plenaries	Neighborhoods, themes (including civic issues)	Neighborhood + Thematic + actor-based, preference for excluded groups (congress)
	6. Oversight and control of execution	Executive	Non-specific commissions (PB Councils, associations)	Specific commissions (Cofis, Comforça, etc.)
PARTICIPATORY (local government)	7. Degree of information sharing and dissemination	Secret, unpublished	Limited dissemination, web, official bulletin, informing delegates	Wide dissemination, including house-to-house distribution
	8. Degree of completion of approved projects (within two years)	Less than 20%	20% to 80%	Over 80%
	9. Role of legislative branch	Opposition	Passive, non-participation	Active involvement
II. FINANCIAL AND FISCAL	10. Amount of debated resources	Less than 2% of capital budget	From 2% to 100% of capital budget	100% of capital and operating budgets
	11. Municipal budget allocation for functioning of PB	Municipal department/team covers costs	Personnel and their activities (i.e. travel)	Personnel, activities, dissemination, training
	12. Discussion of taxation policies	None	Deliberation on tax policies	Deliberation on loans and subsidies
III. NORMATIVE / LEGAL	13. Degree of institutionalization	Informal process	Only institutionalized or only self-regulated annually	Formalized (some parts regulated) with annual self-regulation (evolutionary)
	14. Instrumental or participatory logic	Improvement in financial management	Ties with participatory practices (councils, roundtables)	Part of the culture of participation, participation as right (i.e. San Salvador)
	15. Relationship with planning instruments	Only PB (no long-term plan exists)	Coexistence of PB and City Plans, without direct relationship	Clear relationship and interaction between PB and Planning in one system (ex. a congress)
IV. PHYSICAL / TERRITORIAL	16. Degree of intra-municipal decentralization	Follows administrative regions	Goes beyond administrative regions	Decentralization to all communities and neighborhoods
	18. Degree of investment	Reinforces the formal city	Recognizes both formal and informal city, without preferences	Priority investment in most needy areas (peripheral, central, rural)

Graph 2 Dimensions and variables for differentiating self-denominated PB experiences *Source: CABANNES, 2004. Concept paper on Participatory Budgeting, UN Habitat, Urban Management Program*

analysis table will be illustrated in the example of Rosario [file 10] where the profile of the city is established.

3. Underlying rationale of participatory budgeting[4]
Political projects and ambitions that underpin the vast diversity of participatory budgeting throughout the world can be classified using the following typology.

Budget management tool: PB aims to improve effectiveness and optimal use of resources. It is a technocratic management response to any given fiscal and financial situation. The interest here is in *management.*

Societal governance tool aimed above all at forging social links. In these cases, the underlying interest is to build or rebuild communication and trust between citizens and government. In contexts of disillusionment, disenfranchisement, dissatisfaction, mistrust or rejection of mainstream politics, participatory budgeting can be used as a method to forge a link among actors that transform the city. The primary interest here is *good governance.*

To radically 'democratise' democracy: the interest here is to allow citizen power to be developed and to empower citizens to use that power to make decisions on how public resources should be allocated. The interest in this case is in social and political transformation of society and in building a political system based on participatory democracy.

These three keys to understanding PB are illustrated by the experiences presented.

---

4 This part is developed and illustrated with examples from the article "Contribution of PB to democratic governance", Yves Cabannes and Barbara Lipietz, 2014 for the London School of Economics, London.

No blueprint for Participatory Budgeting. The challenge of diversity.

PARTICIPATORY BUDGETING

FILE
3

BACKGROUND/CHALLENGES

No blueprint for participatory budgeting. The challenge of diversity

Author
Cabannes, Yves
ycabanes@mac.com

Date
27/02/2014 [French]
7/08/2014 [English]
Update 4/2017

One of the characteristics of participatory budgeting processes, such those presented in this book, is the extreme diversity of experience and context. PB must be adapted to specific local situations and political environments, existing social forces, budgets and levels of resources, the number of inhabitants, and the scale at which they organise and operate: village, infra-municipal, city, metropolitan or regional. By putting the thirteen diverse experiences presented in this book in perspective, we can shed light on the wider world of participatory budgeting.

These experiences are only the tip of an iceberg that is largely unknown. Drawing general conclusions would be risky as there is no single, universal model that can be transposed or duplicated. The experiences presented here, however, indicate that each process is creatively reinvented at the local level based on a few simple principles. This analysis focuses on elements of differentiation, illustrated through a series of images. Experiences shown are from all continents where participatory budgeting is in operation. It should be noted, however, that until quite recently there was no PB experience in Arab world, but since 2013 some Tunisian and Moroccan cities have started and are gradually expanding in numbers.

It should also be noted that the experiences presented do not mirror the number of experiences in each region, but rather their quality and their contribution to "Another city is possible!", the theme of this series. The experiences presented in Image 2 show the various sizes of cities in which participatory budgeting

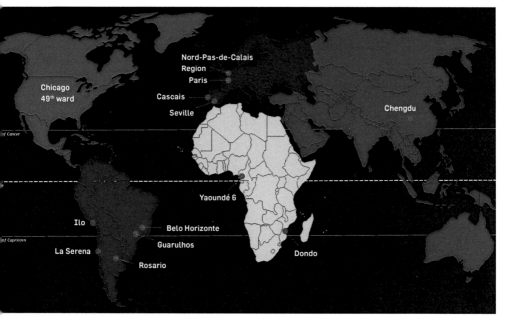

ation of PB processes presented in the book *Source: Cabannes, 2017*

operates. However, there are also PB experiences in cities with fewer than 20,000 inhabitants, considered to be average size in Europe, but considered tiny by Latin America or China's standards. This book does not include examples of PB budgeting in rural areas, villages or in other small cities, which can be found in several regions. However references to films and books are given in the resource section at he end of the book. It should be noted, however, that it is not population size in itself that determines the nature of the PB experience, but rather it is, amongst other things, determined by the type of local authority, the level of available resources and the municipal management structure in place.

Nine of the thirteen PB experiences presented operate at the city level; indicative of the most widespread type of PB found around the world. Two experiences reflect other widespread dynamics, at the "infra-municipal" level such as in the case of District (Ward) 49, Chicago, that elects an Alderman; a District City Councillor, who is a member of the Chicago City Council. *"Communes d'Arrondissement"* in Cameroon, such as Yaoundé 6 also belong to this level of local government, elected by citizens. Some of the cities in this book, such as Rosario or Paris operate at both city and district levels where the larger share of the PB resources will be spent.

Population (Millions)	EUROPE & EUA	ASIA	AFRICA	BRAZIL	OTHER LATIN AMERICA	TOTAL
> 10		Chengdu				1
1 - 4	Nord-Pas-de-Calais Paris			Belo Horizonte Guarulhos	Rosario, ARG	5
0,5 - 1	Seville					1
< 500 000 > 100 000	Cascais		Yaoundé 6		La Serena, CHL	3
< 100 000 > 20 000	Chicago 49th Ward		Dondo, MOZ		Ilo, PER	3
< 20 000						0
TOTAL	5	1	2	2	3	13

Table 1: Over-representation of large cities and very few villages and small cities

Chengdu, the capital of China's Sichuan Province provides an example of a PB experience implemented at the level of a Metropolis. However the case will be "limited" to 5 million people living in 2300 localities and villages in the non-urban districts of the wider metropolis comprising at least 17 million inhabitants.

Participatory budgeting in secondary schools in the Nord-Pas-de-Calais region, France, is a rare example of a PB experience at the provincial and regional level. The originality of this process lies in limiting the participatory budgeting to all types of secondary school and not to opening it to the population at large.

Grasping the multiple scales at which PB operates is critical to understanding the diversity of the PB experiences. Each step on the scale corresponds with a political level, which has specific prerogatives and budgetary responsibilities. Regional authorities are responsible for the budgets for the secondary schools in the Nord-Pas-de-Calais region in France, whereas basic infrastructure is a priority for Mayors' Offices in Peru, which explains why this is the most debated issue in Ilo. This is key for understanding another reason why there cannot be one universal model of participatory budgeting.

FILE 3 · NO BLUE PRINT FOR PB. THE CHALLENGE OF DIVERSITY

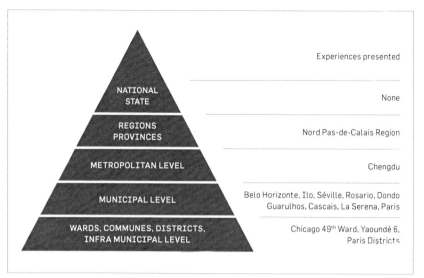

Table 2: Experiences at different spatial scales

The examples in this book present an overview of majority of participatory budgeting processes: classified by their territorial/spatial nature as defined in file 2, i.e. the spatial-political scale at which the experience exists and operates.

Table 3 shows that three cities, La Serena, Rosario and Seville, have what can be classified as mixed systems, with specific resources allocated for specific social groups (see files) and as well as being for specific neighbourhoods. Finally, Cascais, Guarulhos, Belo Horizonte, Paris and Chicago have are examples of a different mixed system, with one portion of their resources and projects allocated spatially (neighborhoods, districts, municipal regions) and another portion allocated for specific sectors (themes). Belo Horizonte has separated its PB for housing, i.e. its thematic PB process, from its participatory budgeting based on administrative regions and regional processes. They are managed alternately and each has its own rationale and administrative anchoring.

One of the drawbacks of this graph is that it presents the situation at a fixed point in time, and does not capture the evolution of PB. For example, at one point the Participatory Budgeting for Housing process in Belo Horizonte

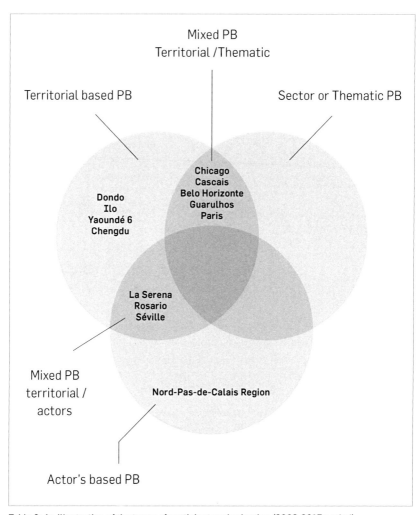

Table 3: An illustration of the types of participatory budgeting (2009-2017 period)

almost disappeared completely. As a consequence, PB in Belo Horizonte is no longer a mixed system (territorial and thematic).

And so how does this relate to the question of whether or not this is a system to promote alternatives to the city as a commodity? It appears that by seeking a model that combines actor-based, thematic and territorial aspects of PB i.e. at the intersection of the three circles, with resources that are clearly defined for each classification, one might find an alternative. This would allow for greater mobilisation of a broader spectrum of citizens. In effect, those participating in improving their neighbourhood (generally belonging to community based associations and struggling for immediate and very localized interests), are generally different from those engaging in a specific sector, for instance belonging to housing struggle movements in PB for Housing, or those exercising their rights as a specific vulnerable groups such as youth, women, or LGBT]. It appears that Rosario could be a pioneering city at this level and there are others considering this approach.

5. Enormous disparity in resources being debated

Very little research on participatory budgeting gives sufficient importance to the financial and budgetary dimension of these processes; research usually focuses on the political and sociological dimensions. However, alternatives to the city as a commodity and building of "other possible cities" also depends on the volume of resources controlled by citizens. The ratio used here to put PB experiences into perspective is the total amount of the budget in US dollars to the number of inhabitants in a city, metropolitan area or region. One of the challenges is obtaining information on the budget over a sustained number of years. A second challenge is that most information refers to the budget being debated and not the budget that will actually be spent which in most cases is significantly smaller. Cities often face difficulties in spending their allocated resources for PB, and this is particularly true in the first years it is implemented. A third challenge is that these amounts vary from year to year. In spite of these constraints, monitoring of approximately 200 experiences since their inception shows that the amount being debated varies tremendously from one case to the other. And those that are best known and most popular are not necessarily those with the highest ratio of resources being debated per inhabitant.

The thirteen experiences in the book reflect the overall disparity of the experiences and the range of resources, inhabitants and years being debated. At one end of the spectrum is Ilo, Peru, with more than $200 per inhabitant per year being allocated through PB mechanisms. This exceptional situation stems from three factors that are also relatively uncommon. Firstly, Ilo debates 100% of its investment budget. Secondly, Ilo benefits from "canon minero", a redistribution of royalties allocated by central government to mining cities, including not only mining cities but also those that process materials extracted, such as Ilo, which processes copper. Thirdly, Ilo is a relatively small city, with less than 70 000 inhabitants, that enjoys a high income per capita.

Only one city, Guarulhos, allocated between $100 and $200 per inhabitant per year in 2011 & 2012. The situation in this city is also unique due, in part, to it being at the same time a wealthy city in São Paulo Region, and at the same time one of the most extreme examples of socio-spatial inequality seen in Brazilian cities. The second reason stems from its capacity to mobilise federal resources for programmes and projects that are priorities for citizens. This was the case, for instance, for housing programmes that receive significant resources during the first half of the 2010's decade. The fact that the city is able to attract such resources from federal government and from São Paulo State Government, thanks in part to citizens' mobilisation through PB, is extremely important in building "other possible cities".

Paris comes next, with an allocated amount of resources in 2016 and 2017 in the range of $50 per inhabitant per year. The portion of this significant amount that is actually spent is still to be defined and is growing swiftly.

Chengdu, Seville and Belo Horizonte are in a fourth category in which between $20 and $30 per inhabitant per year is allocated, but there are significant variations from one year to another. In the case of Chengdu, figures include additional public resources that are topping up those originally earmarked for PB. These levels of resources (between 20 and 30 $/inh/year) are much more commonly found and allow for significant urban transformation in just a few years.

A fifth category includes cities that debate resources of between $10 and $20 per inhabitant per year, such as Cascais, Portugal; Dondo, Mozambique and Chicago's District 49. Once again, within this category, there is great variation. Cascais only allocates a small percentage of its budget to PB (€1.5 million and up to €2.2 million in recent years), although at the national level the figure is high. On the other hand, Chicago's District 49, allocates almost all of its resources ($1 million) to PB. Dondo, is a relatively special case as it is a city of average size that has managed to channel international aid toward projects decided on by its citizens: 50% of the money invested is from the budget and the other 50% comes from external resources.

Rosario and La Serena, Chile were found at the other extreme of the spectrum with less than $10 per inhabitant per year, but in 2016/2017 Rosario has significantly increased its level of resources to PB, reaching close to $ 30 / inh / year. Yaoundé 6 and the Nord-Pas-de-Calais region allocate less than $1 per inhabitant per year. Some comments and observation can be made about these figures. Resources for cities in Chile are, like those in Argentina, very limited, as budgetary resources are concentrated at the national level (Chile) or provincial level (Argentina). As a result, limited resources can be debated at local level. The situation in cities in Cameroon is indicative of African cities that generally lack financial resources. Yaoundé 6 therefore depends on its ability to mobilise both external resources, as Dondo has achieved, and in-kind contributions from its citizens.

It is difficult to compare the example of PB in secondary schools with the other cases as the budget is relative to the number of secondary school students as opposed to the region's 4 million inhabitants. Each secondary school benefits in theory from €100,000 (approximately $106,000 at 2017 first quarter rate of exchange) for its PB process; a significant sum of money. Calculated in relation to the number of secondary school students and not to the population of the region as a whole, the figure is similar to that of Guarulhos, Brazil.

Part 2

CASE FILES

"Real money for real people": Participatory Budgeting in 49th Ward, Chicago, United States

"Real money for real people": Participatory Budgeting in 49th Ward, Chicago, United States

Author
Cabannes, Yves
ycabanes@mac.com

Acknowledgements
This data sheet draws upon
Cecilia Salinas' documentation
of experience prepared for
GOLD report, Contribution
of PB to the delivery of basic
services (Cabannes, Nov
2012). The author expresses
his gratitude to Alderman Joe
Moore, Maria Hadden, Josh
Lerner and Thea Crum for their
comments and for facilitating
the documentation process.

Date
2014

Contacts

Alderman Joseph A. Moore
49th Ward Office, Chicago
joe@joemoore.org

Cecilia Salinas
Participatory Budgeting
Coordinator, Alderman
49th Ward Office, 7356 N.
Greenview Ave., Chicago,
IL 60626. Tel: 773-338-5796
cecilia.salinas@
cityofchicago.org

Maria Hadden
The Participatory
Budgeting Project
maria@
participatorybudgeting.org

Thea Crum
Great Cities Institute -
Neighborhoods Initiative.
Illinois ResourceNet
tcrum3@uic.edu

49th Ward in Chicago: a good example of "infra-municipal" participatory budgeting.

Chicago Metropolitan Area comprises around 9 millions inhabitants; 2.6 million of which live in the 50 Wards of the City of Chicago. Participatory Budgeting started in 2010 in the 49th Ward, which has around 55 000 inhabitants. This was a pioneering process in the USA, usually referred to as PB49, which continues today and interestingly, has been replicated in three other Wards in the past couple of years. It is presented in this book along with Yaoundé 6 as a good example of infra-municipal Participatory Budgeting that is *thematic,* with about half of the resources devoted exclusively to street resurfacing, and the other half pre-assigned to eligible projects such as sidewalk repairs, community gardens, dog-friendly areas, public murals or bike lanes. PB49 is also *territorial;* seven to eight open assemblies take place throughout the ward. (See picture 1, Location map.)

"One of the most racially, ethnically and economically diverse communities in the nation".

These words from the Alderman who championed the process summarise a key challenge facing this district that includes both predominantly middle class and much poorer and ethnically diverse areas. Whilst White American citizens are still the dominant ethnic group, making up 39% of the total population, Hispanic represent 24%, non-Hispanic black 27%, Asian 7% and 3% are classified as "multi-racial". As far as Participatory Budgeting is concerned, the Alderman summarises: *"The main challenge that we faced, and still continue to face, is making sure that public participation in the process reflects the diversity of our community."*

However, the challenge goes beyond inclusive participation, towards social and spatial justice, in case Participatory Budgeting is likely – or not! - to contribute to a fairer spatial distribution of limited public resources.

Highlights of a multi-dimensional process.

Each Ward in Chicago receives $1,3 million in discretionary funds, transferred from central government, to be used for infrastructure improvements. The amount allocated through Participatory Budgeting stabilised at $1 million per year from 2011 to 2013. The amount under discussion represents $18 per inhabitant per year, a relatively high figure in international standards, but obviously small when compared with Chicago's overall budget ($8.2 billion in 2013, equivalent to $3153 per inhabitant per year).

The number of participants in PB49 remained significant over the years, with some variations: from 1980 people in 2010 it decreased in 2011 to 1232 and went up again in 2012 to 1769 participants.

From an institutional perspective, a *Leadership Committee* was specifically set up comprising volunteers, who usually started as community representatives but who chose to take on more responsibilities as they became more involved in the process.

An important aspect of this case is that participatory budgeting is not consultative or advisory but a "power to people" process - ballots are final! In this sense it is radical in relation to many more processes that are simply consultative exercises.

PB49 is an informal arrangement decided at Ward level. Its operating structure is relatively simple: (i) First the elected Alderman leads the

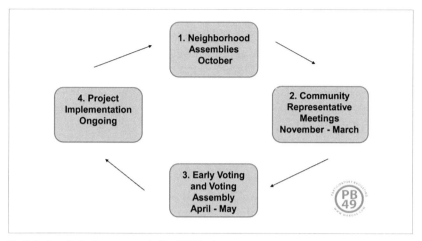

1. Neighborhood Assemblies October

2. Community Representative Meetings November - March

3. Early Voting and Voting Assembly April - May

4. Project Implementation Ongoing

Participatory Budgeting process in the 49th Ward

process and one person in his office (of six), acts as the Coordinator; (ii) Second, *PB Project*, a New York based non-profit organisation has a locally-based qualified PB professional, who comes from the Chicago community; (iii) Third, the whole process relies a lot on volunteers' active engagement at various levels. *"Meeting attendees are encouraged to volunteer as "community representatives"* to develop the most promising projects. (Schugurenski, 2012). In 2012, Community representatives could join one of five project committees: Arts & Innovation; Bike, Walk & Transit; Streets; Parks & Environment and Spanish speakers may opt to join a separate Spanish language committee"; (iv) The Great Cities Institute from University of Illinois plays a monitoring and evaluation role and feeds back the process.

Transparency of public spending: still a challenge.

There is no specific institution responsible for oversight of the implementation of approved projects, as is sometimes the case; instead, the Ward Office is primarily responsible, with the help of some community members. In order to keep the process transparent, *"Every month the Ward Service Office reports the status of all the projects at the Leadership Committee meeting and then the information is made public through the Ward's Website"* (see the site).

A relatively simple annual cycle with four major steps

The process is tailored to a fiscal year that starts in August: (i) Neighbour-hood Assemblies usually take place in October/November. The purpose of which are to gather proposals, which can number 200 to 300; (ii) Community representative meetings from December to February scrutinise the projects, with Ward staff to assess eligibility. Each one of the five committees will meet in order to prioritise usually between 1 to 5 projects; (iii) A second round of neighbourhood assemblies takes place usually in March followed by (iv) a vote by any Ward resident late April or early May either at the ward office or other neighbourhood locations; (v) Lastly, project implementation starts.

Innovations in participation leading to innovative modes of local governance

For Cecilia Salinas, 49th Ward Coordinator of the program, "*The main innovative feature is the involvement of the community in budgeting decisions.*"[1] Very clearly this experience is radical, for the USA particularly but also beyond, in terms of its direct and participatory democracy and contribution to citizens empowerment. A second innovation taken by the steering committee was to lower the voting age from 18 (official in the US) down to 16, in order to encourage young people's participation. A third innovation was to open the vote to ward citizens, regardless of their status, which means that undocumented residents could have their voices heard. The "Governance" model set up seems quite interesting, with a good mix of legislative power (all Ward Aldermen compose Chicago City Council), with operative capacity (Alderman Office), community-based anchoring, with a key role played by *PB Project*; Projects Committees composed of citizens, support from University and significant number of committed volunteers. In order to prepare for future developments it would be useful for further enquiry into how the model PB49 model has evolved over the years and how it overcame tensions inherent in the process. This is particularly relevant since the White House publicly announced on December 6th 2013 that it will be promoting Participatory Budgeting as part of its new Open Government National Action Plan.

---

1 Unpublished data sheet, 12/17/2012.

Underpass mural at Greenleaf, PB funded project. © 49th Ward, Chicago

Projects that suit immediate expectations at micro neighbourhood level

The projects voted for, beyond street resurfacing, over the last three PB cycles, even if limited, reflect the priorities of residents at a micro level, and grounds the process in their day-to-day needs. The list of approved projects below give a sense of how Participatory Budgeting in Chicago was able to adapt to immediate expectations:

2012: 4 sidewalk sections for repair; underpass murals; Plant 139 trees and partial funding for new park playground;

2011: 4 bike lanes, modification of intersection, bike racks; viaduct improvements, partial funding for new playground and beach path extensions.

2010: 27 sidewalk sections for repair, 3 sets of benches and shelters on

Chicago Transport Authority platforms, 3 bike lanes, traffic/pedestrian signal, artistic bike racks; 2 blocks of street lighting; dog friendly area, community garden, underpass mural; solar-powered garbage containers, convenience showers, completion of paved pedestrian path circling the interior of a park, historical signs.

Delays in implementation – still a serious matter to solve.

So far 13 projects have been fully completed however existing delays in implementation have the potential to erode the confidence people have gained in the process. From a factual viewpoint, 35% of Participatory Budgeting projects approved in 2010 and 85% of those approved in 2011 were not implemented by November 2012. According to Alderman's office: "*Each project takes one to three years to complete. Estimated project costs are subject to change/increase by the City and its sister agencies. The work of utility companies (People's Gas, ComEd, etc.) often delays project implementation. City Budget cuts have reduced City and Sister agency staffing, slowing project completion*" (Alderman office power point: 2012). Delays are quite often the case in new processes as they "*...introduce projects that have never been done before by the City. This means that government officials have to create and implement new methods and procedures to complete them*". Lets hope that the couple of years usually needed to ease out this bottleneck will happen in 49ᵗʰ ward as well.

The challenge of public participation that should reflect the ethnic and social diversity of the Ward.

As expressed before the Aldermen recognises the challenge of "Making sure that public participation in the process reflects the diversity of our community." "*Among those who participated in the process there was an over-representation of white middle and upper class folks*", (Schugurenski, 2012). Preliminary results from Crum's evaluation indicate the same pattern; in one neighbourhood assembly where a survey was conducted, 62% of participants were white, despite making up just 39% of the total ward population. Similarly only 6% of participants were Hispanic despite representing 24% of the total population. Under representation of Black and African American citizens is noticeable as well. This situation might structurally be linked to the limited list of eligible projects so far, essentially

Birds, bugs, butterflies and beauty: underpass mural funded through PB. © 49th Ward, Chicago

related to public works that do not necessarily correspond to the priorities of low-income minorities, who might be more interested for example in child care, security or simply increasing their income.

Efforts have been made to address this issue: one of the seven neighbour-hoods meetings is now held in Spanish, posters for ballots are in Spanish and English and the PB Coordinator is Latin American and bi-lingual. Efforts have still to be made and recommendations from evaluations of the outreach methods are important.

"Based on the preliminary survey findings, we recommend continued use of electronic outreach strategies [largely used today] but increasing person-to-person door knocking and phone banking as a way to further engage in low-income individuals and people of color in the process", (Crum, 2013).

Links and bridges with other alternatives, primarily urban agriculture and Community Land Trusts

As in Seville and Rosario, urban agriculture and community gardens are eligible PB projects (see picture 2, Community Garden at Dubkin Park, 49th Ward). It clearly indicates how PB can directly benefit UA. Housing/ Jobs Coops and Community Land Trusts are expanding in Chicago; both promoted by *Community Partners for Affordable Housing* and by the Office for Housing from Chicago Municipality. However Participatory Budgeting and Community Land Trusts remain distinct, operating in parallel. Despite mutual recognition by representatives of both processes, PB and CLT initiatives could benefit greatly from greater dialogue, establish stronger links.

References

ALDERMAN'S Office, 49th Ward. **Data Sheet for GOLD project,** Nov 2012.

ALDERMAN'S Office, 49th Ward. Power Point, Nov 2012.

SCHUGURENSKI, Daniel, **Working Together in the City That Works,** www.shareable.net/blog/the-city-that-works-works-together-participatory-budgeting-in-chicago, 01/04/2012

BIEWEN, John, **Chicago Ward Gives Budgetary Power to the people,** May 26, 2012.

CRUM, Thea. **Preliminary Evaluation Results,** May 2013, Unpublished note.

SALINAS, Cecilia, **Contribution of Chicago 49th Ward Participatory Budgeting to the delivery of basic services,** unpublished note, 2012.

Websites

On Chicago PB: pbchicago.org

Non profit organisation PB Project: www.participatorybudgeting.org

Recommended documentaries and videos

You Have a Date with Democracy: www.youtube.com/watch?v=01bouQJK25Q

Participatory Budgeting in Chicago's 49th Ward 2012: www.youtube.com/watch?v=oe-nbxsmjYw

From Agenda XXI to Participatory Budgeting: the Cascais experiment in Portugal

VOTE OP 16

PARTICIPATORY BUDGETING FILE 5 CASE FILES

From Agenda XXI to Participatory Budgeting: the Cascais experiment in Portugal

Author
Cabannes, Yves
ycabanes@mac.com
Delgado, Cecília
cmndelgado@gmail.com

Acknowledgements
Thanks to the Cascais Agenda
XXI Working Group, especially
Paula Cabral, Nuno Piteira
Lopes and Pedro Jorge Marinho.

Date
2014

Website
www.cm-cascais.pt/
orcamentoparticipativo2012

Videos

Summary of the 9 public
participation sessions in 2012:
www.youtube.com/
watch?v=q1TSU6_Ekxk&featu
re=share&list=PLB6B2118F8
1DD01AC

Presentation of proposed
projects, 2012:
Project 01
www.youtube.com/watch?v
=9fMkrCqQh_Y&feature=sha
re&list=PLaK9AKcKtriG6Zz3
Qo_yE5hzVrHpJXDOj
Project 03
www.youtube.com/watch?v=U-
fZ16n98mQ&feature=share
&list=PLaK9AKcKtriG6Zz3
Qo_yE5hzVrHpJXDOj
Project 04
www.youtube.com/watch?v=
T485KHVT8yQ&feature=sha
re&list=PLaK9AKcKtriG6Zz3
Qo_yE5hzVrHpJXDOj

Agenda XXI started the city of Cascais, Portugal in 2006, and from this process emerged a proposal for Participatory Budgeting, which has been coordinated since 2011 by the municipal team, which is in charge of implementing Agenda XXI. This origin explains to a large extent the importance of environmental issues within the proposals and projects submitted for voting.

Unlike many other municipalities in the Lisbon Metropolitan Area, Cascais enjoys a relatively large resource base: with a population of 206,000 in 2012, and a municipal budget estimated at 202 million Euros annually, the municipal budget averages around 1,000 Euros per resident (Cabral and Marinho, 2012). The Participatory Budgeting process in Cascais is both *territorial [or space based]*, taking place in the city's six districts (called *freguesias* in Portugal), as well as *thematic*, since it addresses the five pillars of the sustainability strategy of Cascais: territory with quality of urban life, territory of creativity, knowledge and innovation, a territory of environmental values, a cohesive and inclusive territory, and a territory of active citizenship.

Confronting citizen's lack of trust in politicians and public officials

The people's lack of confidence in its politicians in Portugal, and in Europe in general, has gotten worse in response to the profound crisis that the country is going through. Nelson Dias (2012b) says that "Portugal has a low level of trust; one of the main objectives of the PB is precisely to win over the trust of the people." Cascais has also faced this challenge, and we will look at the results it has obtained below.

Some singularities of participatory budgeting in Cascais

As for the size of the budget itself, 1.5 million Euros were allocated annually to the process, which is approximately 3.5% of the municipality's capital budget. However, in 2011 and 2012, the municipality increased this amount to 2.2 million, or 5.5% of municipal investments and equivalent to 10 Euros per inhabitant per year, a significant number, even if modest in relation to the overall municipal budget.

A dual system of participation: assemblies and voting, without an elected council

In order to understand the "participatory" part of the process, we must make a distinction between the participants in the assemblies who show up in person to propose and discuss projects, and those who vote on how to prioritize the eligible projects. The average number of participants in the meetings held during the two years of Participatory Budgeting was 461 people (Agenda XXI - Cascais, 2012), which is a relatively low number for a city of over 200,000. Nevertheless, during the election phase, 23,198 people cast their votes in 2012, or 11% of the total population, a very significant turnout that demonstrates the momentum of the process. In 2011, voting could be done at physical polling places, over the phone or via internet. In 2012, votes were only cast by cellular phone, in the form of a free SMS (1 vote per telephone number). It is noteworthy that in Cascais, there is still no "Participatory Budgeting Council" comprised of delegates elected through assemblies, which is very common in other countries, especially in Brazil.

Participation beyond the city limits

One of the unique and extremely positive aspects of the Participatory Budget in Cascais, is that it is not limited, as in the vast majority of PB processes in the world, exclusively to registered residents, or voters within the municipality. On the contrary, "Participation is open to all citizens over the age of 18 who have some relation to municipality of Cascais, whether residents, students, workers, or representatives of the trade movement, private sector representatives and other civil society organizations" (Câmara Municipal de Cascais, 2012). This is an important conceptual shift in the perspective of an open city, inclusive of those who use the city, and not just those who live in it.

An annual cycle organized into 5 stages

The process in Cascais can be considered to be classic participatory budgeting: (1) February – May: the team in charge prepares the process; (2) June – July: participatory public meetings are held to gather proposals; (3) August – September: the proposals are analyzed by the responsible municipal team; (4) October: the proposals are voted on; (5) November: the results are publicly announced (see figure 1).

Transparency in eligibility criteria

The participatory budget in Cascais is based on the values of participatory democracy, contained in Article 2 of the Constitution of the Portuguese Republic. It establishes a model of participation of a *deliberative* nature, in which participants can present proposals and decide on the projects that they feel are the highest priority, according to article 3 of the Rules of Participation (Câmara Municipal de Cascais, 2012). One unique aspect of the process is the clarity and transparency of the eligibility criteria that are used to select the proposals that can ultimately be voted on from among all of the projects that emerge from the participatory assemblies. There are six such criteria (Câmara Municipal de Cascais, 2012):

(a) Proposals must fit within the legal responsibilities of the Municipality;

(b) There must be a defined area of influence, for example the neighborhood that is going to benefit;

(c) The project must be an investment. Events and awareness-raising efforts are not included;

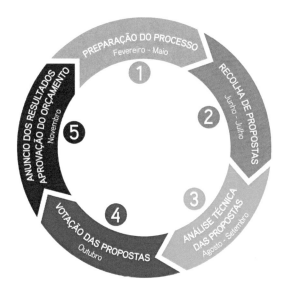

Figure 1: Participatory Budgeting Cycle *Source: Boletim de divulgação do Orçamento Participativo de Cascais*

(d) Total cost cannot be more than 300,000 Euros per project;

(e) Project duration cannot be more than 24 months;

(f) At least one of the five pillars of the city's Sustainability Strategy must be included. This criteria is particularly important, to the extent that it brings together the participatory budgeting dynamic with a vision of sustainable development, in a way that few experiences do.

Innovations, lessons learned and limits

Improving quality of life and services

As a relatively well-organized city, which therefore has a good level of basic services, it is understandable that only 5 of the 30 projects approved for voting in 2011 dealt with basic services, like roads, streets, walkways or avenues, which are generally priorities for participants (Cabannes, 2013). In Cascais, the prioritized projects reflect residents' needs to further improve neighborhoods of illegal originally self built [and called of illegal origin in Portugal], the rural areas within the municipality and local infrastructure, like public spaces, recreation alternatives, community and sports infrastructure, green spaces and cultural facilities. With 8 projects implemented as of 2013, it was very clear that Participatory Budgeting had made an important contribution to improving the quality of life and the places that were "forgotten" by the excluding Portuguese model of urbanization during the era of the neoliberal European illusion. It is also noteworthy that of the 30 projects (2011) submitted for voting, 20 were related to the environment and 5 of these were among the 12 chosen. In 2012, of the 32 projects eligible for voting, 15 were related to the environment, of which 7 were selected as part of the 16 projects ultimately approved.

Paula Cabral, the person responsible for the Participatory Budgeting office in Cascais, and the city's Finance Officer, Nuno Piteira, point to the basic services works as the most emblematic, and highlight the project to provide pedestrian access to Cascais Shopping, selected in 2011, which consisted of lengthening a road to allow for easier crossing and access to the mall, which for pedestrians had been strangled by vehicular traffic (2012a).

Participatory Budgeting, urban agriculture and the environment

One of the central ideas of the "another city is possible" project, is to show the linkages that are formed at the local level between various alternatives. The city of Cascais clearly shows how the participatory budget has been a trigger for developing urban agriculture in diverse, rich ways, as imagined by the people and representatives of community organizations, and not as merely a top-down public policy. The variety of projects submitted for voting in 2012 speaks for itself: a teaching farm, community kitchen and knowledge development workshops; the creation of a community farm; a dog park with green spaces and community gardens, transformation of a rural space with garden into a playground and community gardens.

Limited in-person participation, despite great outreach and mobilization efforts

One of the participants summarized one of the difficulties often cited: "it takes away from time with the family" (Rego, 2011), which demonstrates that participating is perceived of as a loss, and not a gain. To overcome this difficulty, the municipality has made extraordinary efforts to disseminate information about the projects to be voted on and the possible benefits for

of the nine PB sessions, in which 504 people participated. © Courtesy of Cascais Municipality

residents: facebook, illustrated pamphlets, street theater, informational meetings, publicity in supermarkets, interviews with newspapers and meetings posted on YouTube (see website references below). One of the results of the evaluation of the process carried out by surveying participants (Agenda XXI - Cascais, 2012) indicates that the main channel through which they are informed of the Participatory Budget is through "friends", with 130 responses, followed distantly by the internet with 70 responses, and "posters", at 60. These results indicate that interpersonal relationships, and most likely social networks, are more effective than conventional means of communication.

In light of the current situation, how can we increase participation in the assemblies?

Improvement of open spaces in low-income housing estates. Example of a project funded through PB. © Courtesy of Casc Municipality

The socio-economic profile of the participating population in Cascais is relatively high compared to the average for the municipality, which raises the question of how many are participating, in addition to who is participating. One common issue in many cities is how to include low-income populations, those with less education, the unemployed and youth. Proposals described in this book point to ideas such as selecting participants through a lottery among all registered voters, or door-to-door outreach, as occurred in the 49th Ward in Chicago to better mobilize African-Americans and Latinos.

Increasing trust in public administration [and in the political system]?
We have seen that one of the possible contributions of participatory budgeting is to reestablish trust between citizens and local governments. The testimonies and visits tend to demonstrate that in the case of Cascais,

trust between public servants and residents has been affected in a positive way. It is still early to draw conclusions about any changes in relationships with politicians. The director of the program feels that "the Participatory Budget helped to bring visibility and recognition to the work done by public officials, and strengthened transparency in local administration, by bringing the citizen closer to decision-makers." (2012a). Other factors are also helping to build this trust:
- The projects that were voted on were actually implemented.
- Volunteers from the municipal technical team serve as moderators in the process, and receive training but are not paid extra for this work.
- Feedback from the process, regular evaluations, surveys of participants, asking them what works and what doesn't;
- Public officials are willing and capable of demonstrating the culture of Public Service.
- The "In Loco" not for profit enterprise brings expert technical support as a contribution from civil society.
- The participatory budget is part of a broader "system of participation": for example, 50 of the people who responded to the survey said that they also participated in Agenda 21, and many belong to organizations with a history of civic engagement. The municipality, for its part, is a promoter of active citizenship practices, and publishes manuals and newsletters for community organizations and the general public.

References

2012a. **Interview with Paula Cabral and Nuno Piteira,** by Yves Cabannes and Cecilia Delgado. Internal document.

2012b. **Interview with Nelson Dias.** Yves Cabannes. Internal document.

AGENDA XXI - Cascais 2012. **Survey and Evaluation of the Participants in Participatory Budgeting Sessions in Cascais.** Agenda 21 Cascais.

CABANNES, Y. (2014) **Contribution of Participatory Budgeting to provision and management of basic services. Municipal practices and evidence from the field** IIED Working paper, downloadable at pubs.iied.org/10713IIED.html

CABRAL, P. & MARINHO, P. 2012. **Guia para a análise de casos do Orçamento Participativo.** Internal document.

CASCAIS CITY COUNCIL (CÂMARA MUNICIPAL), 2012. **Orçamento Participativo de Cascais - Normas de Participação.** 2012.

REGO, L. 2011. **Orçamento Participativo em Cascais. Um marco de expressão cívica e exercício de cidadania.** Boletim Municipal - Cascais elevada às pessoas, Dez. 2012.

Participatory Budgeting for Housing in Belo Horizonte: A path to producing low-income housing developments and self-management

PB for Housing in Belo Horizonte: a path to producing low-income housing developments and self-management

Author
Cabannes, Yves
ycabanes@mac.com
Delgado, Cecília
cmndelgado@gmail.com

Acknowledgements
We would like to thank
Lenira Rueda Tiburcio, as
well as Claudinéia Ferreira
Jacinto, both of whom are
social scientists, for their
contributions and critical
reflections. Lenira Rueda
played a leading role in the
PBH, as Chief of Cabinet of
the Secretariat of Housing in
charge of implementing the
PBH for the municipality. See
brief 23 of this book, PBH in
Belo Horizonte: Achievements
and Limitations, Lenira Rueda].

Date
2014

Websites

portalpbh.pbh.gov.br/pbh/ecp/
comunidade.do?app=portaldoop

portalpbh.pbh.gov.br/pbh/
ecp/comunidade.do?evento
=portlet&pIdPlc=ecpTaxon
omiaMenuPortal&app=por
taldoop&tax=17309&lang=
pt_BR&pg=6983&taxp=0&

Relatively few participatory budgeting experiences are debating initiatives related to the regularization of land tenure, resettlement or the production of low-income housing, or else these issues are rarely brought to light given that they represent a very small number of projects out of the total, as is the case for example in Porto Alegre. Nevertheless, PBs have helped to facilitate access to housing for low-income families. The experience of the Participatory Budget for Housing of Belo Horizonte is probably one of the most original, particularly in the early years, as it paved the way for the production of self-managed housing, and reinforced ties with cooperativism, two areas that are widely debated by grassroots movements.

In light of the quantitative and qualitative housing deficit in Brazil at the end of the 1980s, federal low-income housing policies that were woefully inadequate given the enormous needs, and pressure from social movements fighting for dignified housing, it is particularly instructive to analyze the possible contribution that a municipality can make to find creative solutions. We are focusing our story on the 1996-2004 period, which were the most fertile years, and due to the fact that with the election of President Lula in 2002, the housing issue was again taken up by the national government.

How the participatory budget began, and how the Participatory Housing Budget emerged

In the 1992 elections in Belo Horizonte, the leftist parties, led by the Labor Party, won power in the municipal government, and the grassroots, intellectual and political players designed a municipal housing policy, in order to try to address the deficit of approximately 50,000 housing units facing this city of over 2 million people.

At the same time, following on the experience of Porto Alegre, where the same party had won the previous elections in 1988 and had implemented participatory budgeting, Belo Horizonte adopted the model, and 1994 would be the start of its first participatory budget. The organized housing rights groups were active in the process, essentially demanding land for construction. As noted by Jacinto (2003), of the 49 projects approved in 1994, 9 attended to "homeless" movements that included low-income renters and primarily those threatened with evictions. There was some tension between the participatory budget for projects that would benefit the collective good, such as new facilities or urban services, and projects that would benefit only certain people, such as housing developments. In this context, the municipal administration, with support from the Housing Council and in accordance with the municipal policy, created a sector-specific municipal budget with its own resources, to attend to these demands.

A third element that is important to understand is that self-managed housing had a history in the country, with the influence of the experience of the Uruguayan mutual aid cooperatives in São Paulo, and the housing collectives in cities like Fortaleza, promoted by the housing rights movements, and in particular the MNLM, the National Movement for Housing Struggle and the UMM, the Union of Housing Movements. And for the first time, the production of self-managed housing programs in three or four-story complexes– see photos – became possible options within a participatory budget process. Advisory groups with expertise in mutual aid and collectives were invited to Belo Horizonte to help bring this initiative to fruition.

As a result, more than 6,000 homes were approved, and by 2008, 3,211 homes had been delivered, distributed among 22 housing complexes, and benefitting close to 16,000 people. Of these, nine housing complexes

Belo Horizonte, Brazil. Under the mobilization of the poor, PB inverted spatial priorities of public spending and significan improved low income neighborhoods, on the forefront of the picture. © Cabannes, Y.

were built through self-management, for a total of 1,231 housing units, benefitting 6,000 people. The built area of between 44 and 55 square meters, was far superior and of better quality than what was offered by federal policies until the early 2000s.

The Participatory Budget for Housing is only one of the various models of Participatory Budgeting in place in Belo Horizonte.
The Participatory Budget of Belo Horizonte is today one of the longest-running PB experiences in the world, as it nears its 20th anniversary in 2014. It is different from nearly all of the other experiences, because of the different modalities which over time began to take shape and develop their own dynamics:
- The oldest version is the **Regional PB**, which takes place in the nine regions of the municipality, and which basically deals with infrastructure works, upgrading favelas and low-income neighborhoods, and building public facilities. From 1994 to 1998 it was an annual event, and in 1999 began to be held every two years.
- The **Participatory Housing Budget**, which is what we are discussing here, was created in 1995 and started in 1996, exclusively involving resources to be allocated to housing, initially for families whose income was below five minimum monthly salaries. There are two types that co-exist: low-income complexes built by contractors, which are called publicly-managed, and self-managed developments produced by mutual aid. This is typical thematic participatory budgeting. (See brief 2 on the typology of participatory budgeting).
- The **digital participatory budget**, which began in 2006 and took place again in 2008 and 2011.
- The **City Participatory Budget**, founded in 1999, debates investments in addition to the other PBs, expands the discussion on the entire municipal budget, and sets public policy priorities. It culminates with the Conference of the City.
- The **Children and Adolescents Participatory Budget** is currently under discussion, and will be rolled out in the near future.

The Participatory Housing Budget as part of housing policy
The Participatory Budget for Housing in Belo Horizonte is not an isolated

FILE 6.1 · BELO HORIZONTE, BRAZIL

program. It is part of the housing production efforts of the Housing Policy, which encompasses other programs and instruments, such as the high-risk settlement removal program (PROAS), a land tenure regularization program and "global specific plans" for the participatory planning of the interventions to normalize the status and provide urban infrastructure to *vilas* (low-income settlements).

Within the Participatory Housing Budget, families without a home, organized into associations, decide on priorities in the construction of new residences for low-income families within the homeless movement. The **Municipal Housing Council**, which we will discuss below, reaches an agreement with the municipal government on the rules of the Participatory Housing Budget. To be eligible to participate, families must have a household income of up to five minimum salaries, be residents of Belo Horizonte for at least two years, not own any property, and be part of a homeless coalition. The houses can be built through a public housing program, or by self-management, in which cooperatives receive public resources allocated through Participatory Budgeting, and manage the construction process, including the contracting of technical and social assistance (Jacinto, 2012).

The Municipal Housing System, implementing policy

One original aspect of the Belo Horizonte experience is that from the beginning, there was an institutional framework designed to implement the policy. The Municipal Housing System consists of a governing body, the **Municipal Secretariat of Urban Policy,** two entities in charge of debating and implementing policies and programs, the **Urbanization Company of Belo Horizonte** (URBEL) – directly responsible for the housing projects approved through the Participatory Housing Budget – and the Municipal Secretariat for Housing, on behalf of the **Municipal Housing Council,** which is a deliberative body and therefore makes decisions on policy guidelines, and the **Municipal Popular Housing Fund,** which channels and targets resources for implementing the Municipal Housing Policy.

Three institutions of democratic governance related to the Participatory Housing Budget:

Municipal Housing Council

Comprised of 20 representatives of various segments of society (legislature, unions, businesspeople, municipal officials, etc.) who address housing issues, 5 of which are from the grassroots housing movement. Nevertheless, a steering committee is a collegial body made up of two members of civil society, and two from the executive branch of the municipal government (Navarro et al, 2002), which approves the Municipal Housing Policy and oversees the spending of Municipal Fund resources. In relation to the Participatory Housing Budget, this entity defines the schedule for registering the housing associations, distributing the housing units and organizes the Housing Forum.

COMFORÇA

This is a group of leaders of the organized homeless movement, elected in the Regional Forums of the Regional Participatory Budget, and in the Municipal Housing Forum. It is responsible for accompanying, monitoring and overseeing the execution of the work of the Participatory Housing Budget. Each of the nine regions has its COMFORÇA to oversee and implement its projects, and there is also a Municipal COMFORÇA, comprised of two delegates from each Regional COMFORÇA (18 members in total), and two delegates from the Housing COMFORÇA.

Ethics Commission

A COMFORÇA group, which has the responsibility of auditing and investigating complaints of irregularities in the homeless associations in the selection of families that will be benefitted. It is a unique body in the world of participatory budgeting, despite the fact that ethical values are in many cases the foundations of participatory budgeting.

How the process works

For homeless families, including renters:

(i) Families interested in participating in the Participatory Housing Budget find a housing association to join;
(ii) The calculation of benefits that go to each association depends on the participation of the families in the Participatory Housing Budget Forum.

Therefore, the more families participate in the Forum, the more resources will be allocated to that association.

(iii) Then, the associations hold assemblies in which they vote to select the participating families. This election is done according to criteria and rules established by the association itself, and takes into consideration active participation in meetings, and the needs of the registered families (Prefeitura de Belo Horizonte, 2013).

Relations between the local government and the grassroots

The Municipal Housing Council defines the investments for each housing program (land tenure titling, Participatory Housing Budget, the relocation of families in high-risk areas, etc.). Then the housing associations composed of homeless people are registered, followed by regional meetings, in which the guidelines approved by the Council are presented together with a report the accounts of previous years. Later, the Municipal Housing Forum will discuss the criteria prioritized by the associations, define the number of beneficiary families and homeless associations, and elect the delegates to the COMFORÇAS.

The opinion expressed by João Baptista Viana, resident of the Mantigueira neighborhood, on the tenth anniversary of the Participatory Budget, summarizes in a few words the benefits of the process: *"The main achievement of Participatory Budgeting is the rebirth of the hope of the community, which for many years was neglected by the government. The Participatory Budget is a generous idea that is going to gradually put an end to society's relationship with political patronage."*

Links with alternatives to the city as a commodity

Over the ten years analyzed here, from 1994 to 2004, Belo Horizonte emerges as a city which illustrates in an embryonic and powerful way the construction of "another possible city", and which weaves innovative relationships among the alternatives to the city as commodity: together with the Participatory Housing Budget, the favela upgrading program (part of the Regional PB), the resettlement programs for communities in high-risk areas, the massive land tenure regularization efforts, are all concrete alternatives allowing people to stay in their neighborhood rather than being evicted, which is an issue addressed in the second book of this series called *alternatives to forced evictions*. These programs illustrate the

...nen played a prominent role in self-managed housing PB developments. Here at Parque Jardim Leblon, Belo Horizonte.
...abannes, Y.

central role of the Housing Council as a force for political democratization. The self-managed housing programs are based on community property, which will be the subject of the third book of the series. Meanwhile, the development of urban agriculture within a perspective of food sovereignty, both for the civil society and for the municipality (book 4) is exemplary in Belo Horizonte, and primarily within the areas of action mentioned above. The self-management programs have in turn re-opened the debate about housing and other types of cooperatives (book 5). There is not enough information available yet to tell us whether or not local currencies (book 6) are being created.

Limitations, and overcoming challenges

For a democratic experience that is as unique as the Participatory Housing Budget, and the financing self-managed housing development in response to the requests of homeless movements, there are evidently many limitations that need to be analyzed. Based on our experience with the process, discussions with residents and the available literature, four such limitations stand out:

- A first limitation was moving from mutual aid self built housing to co-management after the houses were built. The model designed for URBEL

Barreiro neighborhood, staircases, pathways and open spaces funded through PB. © Courtesy of Belo Horizonte Municipali

was not always easily accepted. One way of overcoming this limitation was the social follow up provided by the municipality. An evaluation of the experience after 10 or 15 years would be important to learn from the experience and improve the existing co-management rules.

- A second limitation was voiced years ago by the National Movement for Housing Struggle, which said: "*at the current pace, it will take 47 years for the homeless to acquire a home.*" They didn't want to engage very much in the process, preferring to advocate for federal public policies which the Lula government to a certain extent allowed to move forward. Nevertheless, today, the self-managed housing developments are losing their momentum, and the Housing Council has lost a great deal of its capacity for innovation.

works. Barreiro neighborhood, Belo Horizonte. © Courtesy of Belo Horizonte Municipality

- A third limitation is the delays in the implementation of the program. More than two thousand of the homes approved have still yet to be completed, and the significant amount of resources that the federal government placed in the low-income housing program is not solving the issue. Why were successful programs like the Participatory Budgeting for Housing and the mutual aid initiatives not strengthened and replicated, based on a co-management arrangement between the city government and grassroots movements?

- The fourth limitation is that the PHB is today in a de facto holding pattern. This shows that while good governance and the institutionalization of democratic spheres are necessary, there has to be political will on the part of the movements and the elected authorities to sustain the process.

References

JACINTO, C. F. 2003. The experience of the Public Housing Budget of Belo Horizonte: advances, limits and possibilities of a Municipal Housing Policy. International Colloquium on Local Power. Salvador, Brazil.

JACINTO, C. I. F. 2012. Guide for analyzing Participatory Budgeting cases. Internal document.

NAVARRO, R. G., GODINHO, M. H. D. L. & ALMEIDA, R. D. C. 2002. Governance and Urban Policies, Municipal Council, Participatory Budgeting and Housing Policy in Belo Horizonte in the 1990s. Annual Meeting of the ANPOCS, Brazil.

Municipality of Belo Horizonte. 2013. Portal do OP - Como Funciona - Processo de realização do Orçamento Participativo Habitação. [Online]. Available: portalpbh.pbh.gov.br/pbh/ecp/comunidade.do?evento=portlet &pIdPlc=ecpTaxonomiaMenuPortal&app=portaldoop&tax=17311&lang =pt_br&pg=6983&taxp=0& 2013.

Participatory Budgeting for Housing in Belo Horizonte: Achievements and limitations

PARTICIPATORY BUDGETING

FILE 6.2

CASE FILES

PB for Housing in Belo Horizonte: Achievements and limitations

Author
Lenira Rueda Almeida
lenira.rueda@gmail.com

Lenira Rueda played a leading role in Participatory Budgeting for Housing for a number of years as the Chief of Staff in the Housing Secretariat, in charge of the PBH from the municipal side.

Date
December 2013 [Portuguese];
April 2014 [English]

Participatory Budgeting (PB) was implemented in Belo Horizonte in 1993 to address the popular demands for public facilities and infrastructure, and the Participatory Budget for Housing (PBH) followed in 1995, to attend to popular demands for housing. Already in 1993, Belo Horizonte was organizing its Municipal Housing System, establishing the Municipal Housing Council, the Municipal Housing Fund and the Urban Development Company of Belo Horizonte, as the governing body of the municipal housing policy.

Demands for dignified housing have existed since the city was founded, in 1897, when its plans were only concerned with how to house the public officials of the new capital city of Minas Gerais. By the 1990s, its 2.1 million inhabitants were distributed into 280 official neighborhoods and 170 precarious settlements and favelas.

Popular organizing around the issues of quality of life, infrastructure, social facilities and housing conditions, emerged in the 1990s after a century of such demands, and this resulted in the creation of the Participatory Budget. Already in the first edition of the PB, the struggle for urbanized lots and housing improvements resulted in the creation of the Housing PB in the following year. The objective was to expand the supply of shelter, and the rules of the process were clear: homeless families or renters should organize into housing groups, their income should be less than 5 minimum wages, and residence in Belo Horizonte for at least two years. The biannual

PBH forums decide on the distribution of the resources, using criteria of proportionality between the number of participants and the number of housing units planned, resulting in housing units with a choice of building method: self-help and mutual aid or public sector development.

Between 1995 and 2006, 3,425 families benefitted from the PBH, just with municipal resources. 10 housing projects were built by the city, with the administration, supervisions, and public bidding processes carried out by the municipality and passed on to the families indicated by the homeless groups (*nucleos habitacionais*). Another 9 projects were built by the residents themselves. In this process, the politically allied housing groups organized into a housing association, monitored by the municipal government, which signed a cooperation agreement with each one of them. They chose the land, received technical assistance and managed the construction. The land and the resources were transferred by the municipality. Some of the participants worked as salaried employees, and all of the families participated in the management, whether as leaders, in administration, safety, food service, the school, or in light work at the construction site.

In 2003, with the Lula administration, the regulations of the City Statute and the creation of the City Ministry, Belo Horizonte began to receive federal resources for affordable housing. The Solidarity Credit program financed by the Caixa Econômica Federal made resources available for the production of approximately 1500 homes for the PBH. A dozen developments contracted for in 2007 were to be done by self-management and mutual aid. Of these, 7 were completed by the public sector, and another 4 had their families referred to other developments. Problems such as administrative disagreements between the municipality and the housing rights organizations, administrative incapacity, difficulties in payments and the consequent delays in the transfer of resources made the process very difficult. Many families ended up occupying developments that were incomplete due to financial difficulties, and the residents themselves acted as security guards. The Castelo I Development was the last to be completed in November 2012.

Currently, the PBH is on hold. The municipal administration of the City of Belo Horizonte is not cooperating with the negotiations, due to financial difficulties and an absence of political will. From the point of view of

Urucuia/Barreiro self managed housing development in Belo Horizonte. © Courtesy of Belo Horizonte Municipality. Awarded the Gentileza Urbana - IAB, nominated for Habitat II/Istambul.

Fernão Dias self managed housing development was one of the first funded through PB in Belo Horizonte. © Courtesy of Belo Horizonte Municipality.

the municipal government, it is a very expensive policy, in which each housing unit is appraised at R$80,000.00 in addition to the cost of the land, infrastructure and public facilities. The scarcity of available land within the municipality is another aggravating factor. On the other hand, the large number of settlers in informal settlements, favelas and geologically hazardous areas places pressure on the municipality to attend to the demand for quality housing, resulting from the need to relocate families displaced because of public works projects, which would not go through the PBH process.

The creation of the *Minha Casa Minha Vida* (My House My Life) Program by the federal government in 2009, regularized the distribution of housing in the country, but did not address the organization of grassroots movements of Belo Horizonte. In this federal program, the homes are built with resources from the Caixa Econômica Federal - a federal Government banking institution - and the municipalities participated by providing the land and selecting the families, generally by lottery, following the rules of the national financial system.

This makes it difficult to expand the process of housing production through Participatory Budgeting for Housing, since it does not only attend to families organized into associations struggling for a home. However, the housing movement continues to organize families in Belo Horizonte, and it is represented in the Municipal Housing Council, in the oversight bodies of the State of Minas Gerais and the National Council of the City. Negotiations are in process with the Ministry of the City to hire entities in Belo Horizonte to implement the My House My Life Program, with the participation of the municipality.

All of the housing development built through the Municipal Housing Policy incorporate concerns with the physical, social and economic sustainability of its inhabitants. Social services are provided from the start of the production process until one year after the houses are delivered. This is provided in all housing complexes and is called the "post-residence" follow-up. The social work is important, given the characteristics of the target population, which is comprised of families with little education, dependent on public services, and with some level of political organization which helps them to a certain extent to be prepared for dealing with collective issues, like getting along together in their new neighborhood.

During the selection process, families were always concerned with staying as close as possible to their previous residences, however the scarcity of land within the municipality made it difficult to abide by such requests. Even on this issue, in order to ensure the viability of establishing the developments on adequate sites, vertical construction types were used, which helped to reduce the costs of acquiring land and installing infrastructure, but led to increased population density within the buildings.

It is worth noting that for the families taking part in the self-management and mutual aid program, the process of adaptation to their new homes was always more successful, due to their degree of participation in the construction process, which is also one of the main challenges. Just as for all of the developments build by the Municipal Housing Policy, the management of the multi-storey apartments, maintenance of the buildings and of common spaces, living in harmony with family and neighbors, in addition to paying the common expenses, are obstacles to the sustainability of the housing developments.

Another factor that made it difficult for families to adapt to apartment life is vulnerability of living so close to people with a history of violence. The difficulties that families have in adapting to their new context can lead young people to seek out alternative life choices and become involved in marginal activities. This has been a recurring problem in the low income housing developments, and the solutions are very complex. In most cases, only the strong presence of the force of law, whether in the form of the police or in the form of social policy initiatives, can offer possibilities and alternatives to the dead ends created by these situations.

PARTICIPATORY BUDGETING
CASE FILES

FILE
7

Participatory Budgeting in Guarulhos: transforming people to transform the city

Participatory Budgeting in Guarulhos: transforming people to transform the city

Author
Cabannes, Yves
ycabanes@mac.com
Delgado, Cecília
cmndelgado@gmail.com

Acknowledgements
Our gratitude to Kátia Lima,
coordinator of the participatory
budget in Guarulhos since its
beginning, for her contributions
and updated information.

Date
February 2014 [Portuguese]
June 2014 [English]

Website
www.guaru.com/op

"Participatory Budgeting really transforms human beings"

This testimonial given by Marcia Souza de Moura Silva, one of the participants in the training provided by the Paulo Freire Institute to the delegates and councilors of the Participatory Budget in Guarulhos, a city within the metropolitan region of São Paulo, summarizes one of the most important impacts of the process. In Guarulhos, the idea is not just to transform the city by distributing resources in a more socially and spatially just manner, but rather to transform people so that they in turn can transform their city.

Participatory budgeting in Guarulhos began in 1998, and is part of the third generation of cities with participatory budgeting, which emerged when more than 100 cities, basically those led by the Workers Party, elected in the third municipal elections (for the 1997-2001 period) after the end of the military dictatorship, implemented this process, which was quite innovative at the time.

Embracing the Paulo Freire approach to popular education

One of the unique aspects of the Guarulhos experience is the implementation, since 2005, of a massive popular education program in partnership with the Paulo Freire Institute, geared directly toward participatory budgeting. For the Institute, it is also the first time that it has accepted the challenge of

94

icipatory Budget plenary session © Courtesy of Guarulhos Municipality

designing a specific program linked to participatory budgeting. This educational program is aimed at the representatives of the population elected as participatory budgeting delegates or councilors, the team of popular education agents, the internal team of the Participatory Budgeting Department (today with a staff of 11), and the representatives of the Municipal Councils. As is explained in detail in the book "*Orçamento Participativo de Guarulhos: vivências e aprendizados*", ("The Guarulhos Participatory Budget: experiences and lessons"), this educational process "*helped to expand the participation of their representatives in public governmental decisions, gave participants a critical eye with which to view their city, strengthened the principles of citizenship, and encouraged the autonomy of leaders to produce knowledge about public budgeting, public policies, planning public works and services, and civic organizing, among other issues.*"

The pedagogical function of participatory budgeting in connection with popular education

One cannot understand the roots of participatory budgeting in Guarulhos and what sets it apart, without having an understanding of the liberating educational approach inspired by the educator Paulo Freire. The pedagogical function, which can and should be accompanied by programs like that of Guarulhos and highlighted by Frei Betto, philosopher of liberation theology and advisor to social movements in Brazil: *"Participatory budgeting has a pedagogic function, to bring citizens together, demand discernment and a critical spirit of them, reinforce their neighborhood ties, commit them to social justice and expand their perception of the world, so that, starting with the neighborhood, they can understand that we live in a global village, in which the survival of future generations depends, today, on our ability to administer it well, following the practice of the globalization of solidarity."*[1]

We close this part with two comments by participants in the training program: the first clearly points to the radical democratization that persuades without imposing: *"In the Participatory Budget, you have to learn how to negotiate and not try to boss anyone around or impose your views. This is one thing that I learned and it wasn't the staff [of the Paulo Freire Institute] who said it, but they led me to discover it (Marcia Souze de Moura Silva)."*

The testimony from Rosolene Chagas de Santana, also a participant in the training, complements the vision of participatory budgeting as a space for growth both as a social actor and as a human being: *"Participatory Budgeting taught us, delegates and councilors, many things. I think that when we started with Participatory Budgeting, we were thinking one way, but when we got into it, we didn't have any idea how much we would grow as people and as leaders of the community."*[2]

---

1 Extract from a document by Frei Betto, *Valores que Constroem a Cidade: Orçamento Participativo e Trabalho Voluntário*, written for the Closing Ceremony of the project "Participatory Budgeting and Volunteerism", within the framework of the European Union's URB-AL program. Diadema, February 27, 2007. Frei Betto is a writer, advisor to social movements and a Dominican friar. He studied journalism, anthropology, philosophy and theology, and has participated intensively in the political life of Brazil over the past 45 years, and has written 53 books.
2 Guarulhos, experiences and lessons learned. Participatory Budget. 2008.

Designing the training process with the participants, based on an analysis of their reality

There is not enough space in this article to present the methodology and the content. Nevertheless, it is worthwhile noting that the courses are prepared with the participatory budgeting delegates and councilors, and they are not pre-determined or "ready-made". In fact, the process of determining the important topics to be during the trainings through various activities and based on the reality of the city, marks a difference from other training programs. For more details, see *Vivencias e Aprendizados*, 2008, *Formação cidadão, uma experiência singular* the Education Plan of the Paulo Freire Institute[3]. Before briefly describing the main characteristics of participatory budgeting in Guarulhos, we should mention that many cities in Latin America have incorporated the issue of capacity building of community leaders, and the citizenship school into the dynamics of participatory budgeting, such as La Serena, in Chile, which is presented in this book.

Brief introduction to the experience of Guarulhos

Violent contrasts

Guarulhos, with a population of 1.2 million, is a reflection of the economic and social contradictions of many Brazilian cities. On the one hand, it is one of the main economic poles of the country and a part of the São Paulo Metropolitan Region, and is home to the largest airport in Latin America. On the other, it is one of two municipalities in the State of São Paulo with the largest number of *favelas* and land occupations – 378, according to official statistics. The number of *favelas* (data are from the Brazilian Statistics Institute, IBGE) increased by 112.5% from 1991 to 2000, and Guarulhos now ranks fourth among all Brazilian cities in this indicator. It is this context of brutal socio-economic disparities that the participatory budget stands out as an attempt to provide solutions to some of the most basic questions of social inclusion and access to basic services, education, culture and health, within a perspective of human rights, promoted by the mayor Eloi Pieta, who had a long track record in the field of defending human rights.

---

3 Instituto Paulo Freire, Plano de formação Orçamento Participativo Guarulhos 2006 / 2007, n/d, unpublished Project document.

Involvement of communities during the building phase, like here in Guarulhos, means that more works can be done with the allocated funds. © Courtesy of Guarulhos Municipality

A process inspired by the Porto Alegre model, with local adaptations[4]
The Participatory Budgeting cycle is a deliberative process, in other words the participants have decision-making power. It follows the classical budgetary cycle that starts in March and ends up with the City Council vote on the annual budget that includes the projects voted through PB. It has taken place every two years since 2003, after being an annual event from 1999 to 2003. In the *odd* years, the regional plenary sessions are held, and at these meetings, participants elect the regional representatives for the Participatory Budgeting Council and for the Regional Forums. The first training events for the technicians and the educators in collaboration with the Paulo Freire Institute are then held, along with the thematic sessions, the caravan, meetings, etc. and the regional plan of works for the next two years is prepared. This is considered to be a year of training and preparing the logistical structure. In the *even* years, evaluations are done of the work carried out in the previous year, and continuity is given to the work in

4 The majority of these data are from an analysis carried out by Kátia Lima in 2012 (research for the GOLD report on participatory budgeting and access to basic services).

Same road after the end of PB project. Paved roads and alleys are quite often requested by PB participants, and not only in Guarulhos. © Courtesy of Guarulhos Municipality

progress. The internal rules and regulations that will govern the new cycle are reviewed and revalidated. Participation is open and voluntary – in the 8 cycles that have taken place since 1999, approximately 65,000 people have participated: 55,000 duly registered, and 7,000 who did not formally participate but observed the process, without voting.

A mixed Participatory Budgeting Council, with a citizen majority

The Participatory Budgeting Council, which is the final decision-making body regarding the resources that are subject to debate, is comprised of 42 representatives elected during the 21 plenary sessions that occur in each of the regions, and 26 representatives appointed by the Municipal government, for a total of 68 members. In order to be eligible to serve as a Participatory Budgeting Councilor, candidates must: (i) be a resident of the region, and therefore not exclusively in the city of Guarulhos; (ii) be over 16 years of age – in Brazil, 16 and 17-year-olds are able to vote, and beginning at 18, voting is mandatory; (iii) not hold a legislative

A pause during the implementation of a PB project in Guarulhos, that suggests that PB is not only about projects but also conviviality and community exchange. © Courtesy of Guarulhos Municipality

or executive post; (iv) not be an direct or indirect official of the Public Administration. As in most Brazilian cities, the Councilors are elected by the delegates or representatives, who are in turn elected in the plenary meetings, or assemblies: for every 15 people present in the plenary session, one representative is elected for the Regional Participatory Budgeting Forum; if 16-30 people are present, then they elect 2 representatives; from 31-45, 3 representatives, and so on.

One interesting aspect of the process in Guarulhos is that the projects voted on during the plenary sessions are not limited to the "region" [an infra-municipal unit, there are 21 in Guarulhos]: 6 demands are regional and one is for the entire city, and one priority issue is selected from the set of nine pre-established areas: infrastructure; housing and land tenure; health; sports, culture and recreation; education, economic development, job and income generation; safety, social welfare and transportation.

Limited capital investment capacity

In comparison to the enormous existing needs, the city has limited capacity to invest out of its own regular resources (8.83% of the total budget was for capital expenditures in 2011), and it depends on transfers from the Federal Government, for example with the affordable housing program called *Minha Casa, Minha Vida* (My house, My life). Therefore the resources for each of the 21 administrative "regions" in the participatory budget can vary depending on these transfers. Nevertheless, the amounts of resources that have been mobilized in recent years have been very high in international terms, and the works that have been carried out both at the city level and in the regions have helped to reduce disparities. From 2009 to 2011, 217 million Euros (510 million Reals) were allocated to projects – many of them on a large scale – that were discussed and approved through the participatory budget, with significant annual variations: the average over the three years was approximately 60 Euros or US$ 80 per capita per year, which places Guarulhos near the top among cities with participatory budgets.

Strong mobilization and insufficient dissemination

The grassroots mobilization takes place through an intense outreach plan that uses a variety of media, such as a car with loudspeakers, pamphlets, outdoor advertising, announcements in magazines, banners, meetings with leaders, etc. A more recent initiative was to create an awareness-raising novella, or soap opera, with a humorous twist, about the PB, available at the link: www.youtube.com/watch?v=2aJHRmwJOMM. This communicational effort, led by the technical team, explains in part the sustained rate of participation over time. The shortage of dissemination mechanisms continues to be a chal-lenge, despite these efforts: there is one publication and an annual accountability report, but these are not sufficient to inform the public about the results that have been achieved.

One of the ways employed to face this challenge was publishing information in the official newsletter of the Municipality, which reaches the 26,000 municipal employees. In addition, the civil society has been fostering the creation of blogs.

Concluding remark

Despite the challenges mentioned before that remains for the future, Guarulhos continues paving the way towards "another possible city".

Under the impulse from trained PB delegates and councilors and the strong support from the municipality, most probably innovative bridges will be constructed with urban agriculture in a food sovereignty perspective, local currencies or mixed housing / jobs cooperatives.

References

LIMA, Kátia (2012) **Inquérito Gold – Guarulhos e perfil municipal do OP.**

Municipality of Guarulhos and the Paulo Freire Institute (2008), **Participatory Budgeting in Guarulhos: Experiences and Lessons Learned.**

Dondo, Mozambique: a unique example of Participatory Budgeting as a driver of Good Governance

PARTICIPATORY BUDGETING
FILE
8
CASE FILES

Dondo, Mozambique: a unique example of PB as a driver of Good Governance[1]

Author
Cabannes, Yves
ycabanes@mac.com
Delgado, Cecília
cmndelgado@gmail.com

Date
February 2014

Contact
Anselmo Figueira
anselmofigueira@yahoo.com.br

Dondo: one of the first elected local governments in Mozambique

Dondo was one of the first of 33 elected governments created as a result of the law on decentralisation passed in 1997 and 1998. Ten years later, an additional ten were added to the original 33, totalling 43 elected local governments. In spite of the fact that these governments manage a small portion of Mozambique and face immense challenges in one of the poorest countries of the world that suffered a long civil war following a war of independence, a 2008 evaluation indicated that decentralisation had brought positive results, and was here to stay. A second conclusion was that participatory planning and budgeting in Dondo was a highly significant innovation, designed and developed locally, for the promotion of of democracy and the improvement of extremely hard living conditions (Cabannes, 2009; Vasconez and Ilal, 2009). This narrative shortly highlights some aspects of the process and its outcomes.

In 2010 the town of Dondo, located half an hour drive from Beira, the regional capital of the central region of Mozambique, had a population of 70, 000. Beyond the formal town centre that dates back to colonial times, 'cidade cemento' (cement city), Dondo

1 Part of this narrative was published as part of a paper on PB in Africa (Cabannes, Y, in Villes en Développement, March 2010:3, nº 88, pp. 4-5). The primary information was essentially provided by the municipality of Dondo and collected over field visits by author. We would like to express our gratitude to Manuel Cambezo, elected Mayor of Dondo since the beginning of the experience and to Anselmo Martins Figueira (see contact), Director of Finance and Planning at Dondo Municipality. They have been essential in explaining the uniqueness of Dondo process.

comprises ten overpopulated, self-built districts with poor facilities. In addition, rural Dondo counts around fifty villages and hamlets, many of which have poor access, particularly in the rainy season. In 2007, less than 6% of the population had access to water on their plot of land.

Dondo PB is essentially a **"territory based"** system that takes place in a very decentralised fashion. Beyond the ten official neighbourhoods that comprise the city, PB also occurs in 51 communities, called *"unidades comunais"*. These neighbourhoods and communities organise projects around four priority sectors: urbanisation, infrastructure, water sanitation and roads.

Five stages of the participatory budgeting process

1. The first stage consists of a socio-economic diagnosis conducted in each districts by the development units (defined below) with the population and the community councils.

2. Then, the proposed projects and identified needs are divided into three categories: (i) those with local solution, for example cleaning streets or drainage channels; (ii) projects which require mixed solutions that involve both the community and the municipality, for example repairing zinc roofs on schools that require the purchase of nails, whilst the manpower will be from the community; (iii) needs which involve the municipal budget only, for example street lighting. This is a unique innovation amongst PB experiences.

3. Once the communities have defined their priorities, the municipal team call upon its Consultative Forum that finalises the budget related to PB projects, taking into account the anticipated municipal revenue.

4. The conclusions and recommendations of the Forum are presented to the Municipal Council that takes a vote on the proposed budget.

5. The decisions are implemented with the participation of the community

A complex participatory system that reflect the local social and political complexity

Since the start of municipal decentralisation in 1998, a broad-based participatory process has provided a basis for one of the first participatory budgeting processes in Africa. The originality of this participatory system lies in the fact it is based and takes into account the complexity of existing structural conditions:

Municipal Market Samora Moisés Machel funded through PB, Dondo, Mozambique. © Courtesy of Dondo Municipality

- Socio-political structures inherited from FRELIMO, the Marxist party that spearheaded the anti-colonial liberation war and that came into power after independence,
- Chiefdoms and traditional organisations, many of which joined or supported the opposition party, RENAMO, during the post independence civil war,
- And more recently formed organisations, religious and non religious that could be classified as 'civil society'.

Over the years, several bodies and spaces that play a role in participatory budgeting have taken shape:
- Development Units in each district, led by social workers and educators;
- Development Units in each one of the 51 "village" units in rural areas and;
- Community Councils.
- A multi-actor Consultative Forum known locally as *Fórum Consultivo Municipal*, which over years became the final body for participatory budgeting decision making. It is composed of 75 members, consisting of elected representatives from District and Neighbourhoods Development

ting of the Consultative Municipal Forum composed of 75 members from quite diverse sectors from Dondo. © Courtesy of
do Municipality

Units (50 in total), community leaders, religious leaders, mass civil organisations, influential public figures, representatives from the municipality and from local economic sectors.

The process has benefited from the Mayor of Dondo's leadership; his direct involvement explains the steady progress and achievements. From an institutional viewpoint two different administrative bodies coordinate the PB: (i) the Office for Studies and Councils (*Gabinete de Estudos e Assessoria*, GEA) and (ii) the section of Community and territorial affairs (SACT). Both fall under the Administration and Institutional Development Secretariat (*Vereação de Administração e Desenvolvimento Institucional*). This institutional anchoring underlies strong governance logic, both societal and institutionally horizontal, just as in Rosario since PB's inception or in Porto Alegre during the mid-2000s.

A unique governance model locally designed and developed through participating budgeting.

One of the most remarkable aspect of PB in Dondo was the decision to design and to put to work a multi-actor process and governance model, involving

107

Inauguration of community water pump, funded through PB © Courtesy of Dondo Municipality

a broad range of actors immediately addressing historical tensions. PB played a central role both as a process and as a participatory channel 'opener'. The small projects formulated, selected and implemented became the glue that allowed for good governance to work. It is probably one of the most sophisticated governance models to have brought significant change to peoples' lives, for example through the improvement of basic services, over the past decades. It is no surprise that PB in Dondo received the Excellence Award from United Cities and Local Government Africa, UCLGA for their model at the Africities Summit in Marrakech in 2009.

Improvement of living conditions and basic services
Throughout the years 2007, 2008 and 2009, US $2,6 million was invested through PB; approximately half from the local government and half from international aid. This figure is impressive for a poor municipality in one

of the poorest countries in the world. This equates to a value of over US $12 per inhabitant per year, Dondo PB is probably at the top end in relation to the amount of money spent per inhabitant in African PBs so far.

The achievements of this process, in terms of improving in living conditions in only a few years, with limited resources, are outstanding. This is particularly with regards to the improvement of basic services; the provision of an improved water supply; health centres; and the installation of stand pipes. Furthermore community mobilisation has led to a large number of works being conducted including the construction of latrines and drainages canals.

Positive impact and increased confidence between local government and citizens

The impact of participatory budgeting has gone beyond mere budgeting; it has increased communication between municipal employees and the population, For example in regards to measures for living with with HIV/ AIDS and improving security in districts. This is thanks again to the increased confidence the communities have gained in their capacities through the PB process and to the better relations between actors involved.

International aid is a potential risk for a long-term sustainability of participatory budgeting process.

Most of the experiences of participatory governance in Mozambique are funded and in some cases implemented by technical and/or financial international cooperation agencies (Vásconez and Ilal, 2009). Such a financial dependency puts at risk the long-term sustainability of the process, particularly for processes that are not institutionalised.

Despite the end of a project to support decentralization in Dondo, funded by the Austrian North-South Institute, and a project to support Districts and Municipalities, funded by the Austrian Bi-lateral Cooperation Agency, the process of participatory planning, established through both projects, maintained itself in the Municipality of Dondo.

However immediately following the end of the Decentralization Support Project – funded through the Swiss Cooperation Agency, in Cuamba, Metangula, ilha do Mozambique, Montepuez, and Metangula municipalities – the participatory planning process slowed down, and was eventually disrupted in Ilha do Mozambique and Mocímboa da Praia in 2007 and 2008 (Nguenha, 2009). Dondo Municipality's ability to maintain and transform its process, making use of international funds, without being financially or technically dependent makes it all the more significant.

References

CABANNES, Y, **Urban Governance and Planning in Mozambique, in Municipal Development in Mozambique. Lessons from the first decade,** (2009:5), World Bank Report No. 47876-MZ: Washington, pp 79-106, Chapter 3.

ILAL and VASCONEZ, **Urban Governance and Planning in Mozambique, in Municipal Development in Mozambique. Lessons from the first decade,** (2009:5), World Bank Report No. 47876-MZ: Washington.

FIGUEIRA, A. (2010). **Planificação e orçamentação participativa em Dondo, exercicio da democracia participativa,** Documento de Trabalho, 19 páginas, não publicado [comunicação com o autor]

FIGUEIRA, A. (2012). **Relatório Gold - Orçamento Participativo em Dondo.**

NGUENHA, E. (2013). **A Experiência Moçambicana de Orçamento Participativo.** Esperança Democratica – 25 anos de Orçamentos Participativos no Mundo. A. I. LOCO: 125-131.

NGUENHA, E. J. (2009). **Governação Municipal Democrática em Moçambique: Alguns aspectos importantes para o desenho e implementação de modelos do Orçamento Paticipativo.** Comunicação para a II Conferência do Instituto de Estudos Sociais e Economicos intitulada; Dinâmicas da Pobreza e Padrões de Acomulação Económica em Moçambique. Maputo: 30.

PARTICIPATORY BUDGETING

FILE
9
CASE FILES

La Serena, Chile: Participatory Budgeting in neighborhoods and public schools, a true academy of citizenship

La Serena, Chile: Participatory Budgeting in neighborhoods and public schools, a true academy of citizenship

Authors
Juan Salinas Fernández
forochileno@gmail.com
Millaray Carrasco Reyes,
millaray.carrasco@laserena.cl
Hugo González Franetovic
hugo.gonzalez.franetovic@
laserena.cl
(editors) in *Ciudadanos
transformando ciudades. El
presupuesto participativo en la
Serena*, Pages 152 -154

Date
March 2014 [Spanish]
June 2014 [English]

**Coordinators of the Book on
Participatory Budgeting**
Cabannes, Yves
ycabanes@mac.com
Delgado, Cecília
cmndelgado@gmail.com

**Translation from Spanish
to English**
Richard Huber

Website
www.laserena.cl/
presupuestos-
participativos/2013/
index.html

The *comuna*[1] of La Serena, located some 470 kilometers to the north of the Chilean capital of Santiago, has a population of approximately 200,000, and since 2009 has been the site of one of the richest participatory budgeting experiences in Chile. One aspect of the La Serena process that truly stands out is having opened up participation to youth ages 14 and up in the neighborhood participatory budget, which is complemented by the Participatory Budget for Public Schools, which involves all students from municipal educational institutions throughout the entire academic cycle; that is for children aged 6 to 18. Both participatory budgeting initiatives (neighborhood and school) are presented in this article.

A number of distinctive aspects make this experience particularly interesting. First of all, it has a broad institutional base, which helps to mobilize the municipal government as a whole: it brings together the municipal departments of Community Development, Planning, Finance and the City Manager into an Executive Secretariat, which leads the process from the local government side. Second, the rules of the game, called the general terms and conditions, are clear and transparent, and are integrated with a strong website-driven outreach effort, which provides information to the citizens, fundamental elements of success.

Furthermore, a specific committee, the **Territorial Steering Committee** (*Directiva de la Mesa*

---

1 Sub-provincial political and geographic division in Chile, similar to a county

112

...ssembly participants, La Serena, Chile. © Courtesy of La Serena Municipality

Territorial), elected from the territorial working groups of the participatory budget, guarantees a strong popular presence, and also reflects the diversity of the municipality and its regional specificities: rural, pampa, seaside and urban neighborhoods.

From the "open town forum" to participatory budgeting[2]
One space for exercising citizen participation which the La Serena municipality has been implementing since 2009 is the "Open Town Forum" (*Cabildo Ciudadano*), which is held every two years (2009 and 2011). The Open Town Forum is an important moment for interacting, analyzing and discussing issues of public interest, in which social and community stakeholders from the various areas of the *comuna* come together to offer their opinions, suggest ideas and express their demands to authorities and teams of municipal professionals. The result of this work and exchange is

---

2 The narrative that follows has been taken from the book *Ciudadanos Transformando Ciudades. El Presupuesto Participativo en La Serena*, the lead author of which is Juan Salinas Fernandez, with the municipal team responsible for coordination and editing: Hugo González Franetovic and Millaray Carrasco Reyes, under the leadership of the Mayor of La Serena, Raul Saldivar Auger, from 2008 to 2012.

Public school student presenting a project, La Serena, Chile. © Courtesy of La Serena Municipality

reflected in the inclusion of demands in various local policies, specifically in the primary instruments of municipal administration such as the Communal Development Plan (PLADECO) and the municipal budget, among others.

Participatory selection of the name for the "Mirror of the Sun" park

The selection of the name of the current "Mirror of the Sun" Park (*"Espejo del Sol"*), a process which took place in May 2009, marks a milestone in terms of the participation of children and youth of La Serena; it was the first mass participation and voting process to take place in the city. Although it appeared to be a simple process, given its mass participation and social and community impact, truly represented a watershed for child and youth participation in the *comuna*. This voting process also served as the trial run for the first voting in the neighborhood participatory budget process in August 2009.

The process leading to the inauguration of the "Mirror of the Sun" Park managed to rally the entire universe of students in the *Las Compañias* sector, and mobilized the entire educational community. Teachers, school authorities and students took on the challenge with enthusiasm and creativity, which resulted in 146 proposed names for the park. Of that total, 20 were preselected to be on the final list for an unprecedented mass poll to select the best name for the park.

Over 8,000 public school students, from first grade to high school, voted for their preferences in an informed, ordered and transparent act of civic participation. Finally, with more than 2,000 votes, *"Espejo del Sol"* was declared the winning name.

"This was a practical civic education class," concludes former Mayor Raul Saldivar, who above all valued the dynamics and interactions that the experience generated between students, both within the classrooms as well as at home. The analysis of their surroundings, the ways they understand their realities, the mechanisms deployed to foster dialogue and consensus-building, are some of the most valued lessons learned by the students and their teachers and families.

The Participatory Budget for Public Schools, a great innovation

The participatory budget for public schools has been in place for only two years so far (2010 and 2011), however it has resulted in the materialization of 60 projects in the 17 urban and rural municipal educational institutions. Close to 30,000 young people have taken part in the process over this period, analyzing and debating over the allocation of over 47 million pesos. Methodologically speaking, the school-based participatory budget takes place in all educational establishments that are administered by the municipality through the Gabriel Gonzalez Videla Municipal Corporation, which is in charge of public education in the *comuna* and is responsible for 13,000 children between urban and rural schools, as well as institutions that attend to special needs, such as children with autism, blindness or learning disabilities. One of the primary declared goals of the initiative is to integrate the student community, through citizen participation.

Resources mobilized: economic and technical-methodological

For the implementation of the first edition of the Participatory Budget for Public Schools Program for 2010, the La Serena Municipal Council approved a $22,000,000[3] contribution to the Gabriel Gonzalez Videla Municipal Corporation. In addition, there was a transfer of knowledge and experience from the coordination team of the Neighborhood PB to the coordinators of the experience within the Corporation, thus making it possible to transfer and replicate the practices of the neighborhood model to the public schools.

In 2011, the Gabriel Gonzalez Videla Municipal Corporation assumed full control over the implementation of the school-based participatory budget, allocating $25,000,000 from various sources, with excellent results. This was an important step forward in the municipal administration of education, since in addition to internalizing and taking ownership of the process, new non-municipal resources were brought into the system.

Other important resources mobilized include the technical and professional teams necessary to carry out the program. More than 300 teachers, directors and administrators are deployed throughout the entire *comuna* to ensure that all of the phases of the La Serena participatory budget for public schools goes smoothly.

The voice of the students

In its second consecutive year of implementation, the participatory budget for public schools taking place in La Serena is gradually taking root as a good practice for introducing and including young students in public affairs of their interest. In the second edition, the students, armed with a better sense of the initiative, are discovering and experiencing the potential of citizen participation.

The spaces and mechanisms of participation represent a "...democratic forum, in which they can express what they feel in a context of equality, and address problems". They value above all the space that has been opened up and the educational implications that this can have for their development and adult lives: "We are preparing ourselves for when we are bigger and can vote...", they say with excitement. They are also able to observe and highlight the challenges associated with getting involved and participating responsibly, which is in some ways a product of their experience over these two years – "participation goes hand in hand with teamwork; groups of people working together to achieve something for the common good..."

_____

3 1 Euro = 752 Pesos [2014]

ping exercise as part of PB process. La Serena, Chile. © Courtesy of La Serena Municipality

Students say that certain leadership skills are needed to carry out participatory initiatives like this one. Their prior experiences with participation were limited to the organizations of school events or to offering an opinion on a certain subject in particular, however they had never heard about or taken part in a process like the participatory budget. It is a completely new experience for them, and they agree that it has served as a valuable complement to their education, and that they have strengthened their ability to organize and to dialogue with other members of the school community.

A positive valuation of the participatory budget

Within the school community, and specifically among the students, there is a common agreement that the participatory budget has been a very positive initiative. Depending on how students experience the process,

117

PB in Public Schools: La Serena Mayor [standing, with tie] hands over a check to a group of students to fund the project voted for. © Courtesy of La Serena Municipality

they highlight different elements of the process – "... we think that it's good to create places where we can play, we have set times to use the facilities." Others say that it is "... a good opportunity put ideas into practice that otherwise wouldn't get done."

They feel a true sense of pride in what they have achieved, and their role in how the program worked: an orderly and transparent process, which at times required a lot of extra work, but which when seen with some perspective, "...that is one of its advantages."

"...The ideas are ours"

It is obvious that they care about their projects, and forcefully defend their ideas. In response to the mere suggestion that the projects could receive some guidance from teachers and administrators, they are very clear: "... the ideas come from the students. In the student center, they talk about what things are needed, then they design the projects and vote. They are exclusively the ideas of the students..."

The young people are overflowing with ideas that they then have to transform into projects, to be submitted to consideration and debate among their peers. In some cases, they have come up with innovative ideas which are even being replicated by others.

When the ideas are their own and the projects reflect the wishes of the students, the results are better, and the initiative is more sustainable. This has been proven over and over again: "Everyone is very motivated, doing things on their own, like proposing ideas, getting estimates, etc. We are moving a lot around this program..." This enthusiasm, in some cases, continues even after the project is formally ended.

A broad and creative array of potential projects

Since 2010, around 50 projects were consolidated and approved per year (see annex 3, book on the La Serena PB, pp. 152-154), covering a wide, creative range of projects. These included school radio stations, recreational spaces, cafeteria, microwave ovens, bathroom remodeling, ping-pong tables, exercise equipment, dressing rooms and equipment for artistic activities, an electronic school newspaper, starting an instrumental band, purchasing an audiovisual kit, playgrounds, these are just some illustrations of the wealth of proposals that have been voted on.

Beyond the projects

Despite their young age and limited life experience, the students have been capable also of seeing the participatory budget from another perspective, highlighting different facets that they have en-countered along the way, and which go beyond the materialization of their ideas and projects. In their own words, they note that "... The participatory budget has helped us to get organized, the groups get together during recess to talk, it has encouraged unity and dialogue among the students in different grades."

Judging from what students say, the participatory budget, its implementation and the improvement projects that have resulted from it, are generating new dynamics of integration within the school.

References

SALINAS FERNÁNDEZ, F. (org), CARRASCO REYES, M. and GONZÁLEZ FRANETOVIC, H (editors), **Ciudadanos transformando ciudades. El presupuesto participativo en la Serena**, Municipality of La Serena, Available: issuu.com/laserena/docs/libro_pp_la_serena

Municipality of La Serena, **Proceedings from the 4th International Seminar**, 2012, Available: www.laserena.cl/sipp2012

Rosario, Argentina: Presentation of an analytical grid to establish a Participatory Budgeting profile at city level

Rosario, Argentina: Presentation of an analytical grid to establish a Participatory Budgeting profile at city level

This narrative is an adapted extract of a chapter on the democratic contribution of participatory budgeting for a text book for the London Schools of Economics, LSE in London, written by Cabannes, Yves, Lipietz, Barbara, Delgado, Cecília.

Authors
Lipietz, Barbara
b.lipietz@ucl.ac.uk
Cabannes, Yves
ycabanes@mac.com
Delgado, Cecília
cmndelgado@gmail.com

Date
2014

Acknowledgements
We would like to thank Ana Laura Pompei, Coordinator of the Planning and Evaluation team of the Municipal General secretary for her comments and the sharing of her experience and data. Our gratitude as well to Dr. A. Ford, from Rosario University, Faculty of Political Sciences and International Relationships for his insights on the case. The narrative is fuelled by their comments, written source, as well as numerous visits to Rosario from 1999 to date.

Website
www.rosario.gov.ar/sitio/
informacion_municipal/pp.jsp

To help discern amongst the great (and growing) diversity of PBs across the globe, we first present an analytical grid adapted from the grid developed by Y. Cabannes for UN-Habitat (UN-Habitat, 2004: 20-21). This grid has been largely tested in the field and modified over time to reflect the practices of PB in their diversity. It was set up with two key objectives in mind: a) to serve as a tool for building a city's PB profile and; b) as an action tool for devising locally-specific PBs. We present the grid briefly before exemplifying its use in the case of Rosario, Argentina.

Dimensions and variables to build a city's PB profile

The grid comprises of a series of analytical dimensions, derived from extensive studies of PBs in their diversity, and an assessment of the intensity of their implementation. On a *vertical axis* are eighteen variables grouped under four broad dimensions: financial and fiscal; participatory; normative/legal; territorial. A *horizontal axis* is organized along 'minimal arrangements', 'medium arrangements'

ng PB poll to the streets, Rosario city center. © Courtesy of Marcelo Beltrame

and 'advanced arrangements' with each of the arrangements corresponding to the assessment of a particular situation *at a given time.*

As we will see in the case of Rosario below, it is important to note that cities may be "advanced" on some variables and less so on others. Moreover, temporality is an important element to take into consideration when assessing PB experiments since PB processes are evolutionary (they can, and do, change over time). All in all, the grid acts as an analytical tool, helping to draw out the varied contribution of PBs to urban governance in specific contexts and at particular times. It can also act as a barometer of the various political projects underpinning PBs, and as political instrument or lobbying tool to motivate for the irreversibility of PB and the deepening of its transformatory promises.

Highlights on the grid: Rosario PB experience, Argentina

To illustrate the analytical use of the grid, we propose to unpack the experience of PB in Rosario, Argentina, according to the grid categories.

DIMENSIONS	VARIABLES	MINIMAL ARRANGEMENT	INTERMEDIATE ARRANGEMENT	MAXIMUM ARRANGEMENT
I PARTICIPATORY (citizens)	1. Forms of participation	Community-based representative democracy	Community-based representative democracy open to different types of associations	Direct democracy, universal participation
	2. Instance of final budget approval	Executive (partial consultation)	Council (consultative)	The population (deliberation and legislative approval)
	3. What body makes budgetary priority decisions?	None	Existing social or political structure Government and citizens (mixed)	Specific commissions with elected council members and a citizen majority
	4. Community participation or citizen participation	Neighborhood level	City-wide level, through thematic contributions	Neighborhood, regional, and city-wide level
	5. Degree of participation of the excluded	Thematic and neighborhood plenaries	Neighborhoods, themes (including civic issues)	Neighborhood + Thematic + actor-based, preference for excluded groups (congress)
	6. Oversight and control of execution	Executive	Non-specific commissions (PB Councils, associations)	Specific commissions (Cofis, Comforça, etc.)
PARTICIPATORY (local government)	7. Degree of information sharing and dissemination	Secret, unpublished	Limited dissemination, web, official bulletin, informing delegates	Wide dissemination, including house-to-house distribution
	8. Degree of completion of approved projects (within two years)	Less than 20%	20% to 80%	Over 80%
	9. Role of legislative branch	Opposition	Passive, non-participation	Active involvement
II. FINANCIAL AND FISCAL	10. Amount of debated resources	Less than 2% of capital budget	From 2% to 100% of capital budget	100% of capital and operating budgets
	11. Municipal budget allocation for functioning of PB	Municipal department/team covers costs	Personnel and their activities (i.e. travel)	Personnel, activities, dissemination, training
	12. Discussion of taxation policies	None	Deliberation on tax policies	Deliberation on loans and subsidies
III. NORMATIVE / LEGAL	13. Degree of institutionalization	Informal process	Only institutionalized or only self-regulated annually	Formalized (some parts regulated) with annual self-regulation (evolutionary)
	14. Instrumental or participatory logic	Improvement in financial management	Ties with participatory practices (councils, roundtables)	Part of the culture of participation, participation as right (i.e. San Salvador)
	15. Relationship with planning instruments	Only PB (no long-term plan exists)	Coexistence of PB and City Plans, without direct relationship	Clear relationship and interaction between PB and Planning in one system (ex. a congress)
IV. PHYSICAL / TERRITORIAL	16. Degree of intra-municipal decentralization	Follows administrative regions	Goes beyond administrative regions	Decentralization to all communities and neighborhoods
	18. Degree of investment	Reinforces the formal city	Recognizes both formal and informal city, without preferences	Priority investment in most needy areas (peripheral, central, rural)

Table 1 Dimensions and variables for differentiating self-denominated PB experiences *Source: CABANNES, 2004. Concept paper on Participatory Budgeting, UN Habitat, Urban Management Program*

Rosario's grid PB profile is illustrated in Table 2. PB was voted in by the city's Municipal Executive in 2002 and started in earnest in 2003. It has continued uninterrupted ever since.

Starting with dimension I (financial and fiscal dimensions), it is clear that Rosario's PB experiment is an 'advanced' process. Municipal resources debated (variable 1) have increased steadily between 2003 and 2011, from 24 to 36 millions pesos (i.e. roughly 9 million dollars per year)[1], which classifies the city as a 'medium arrangement' on the grid. Rosario qualifies as 'maximum arrangement' in terms of having a specific budget earmarked for PB. The latter has covered the costs of PB personnel, dissemination of PB through posters and the media, training activities, as well as research into innovative ways of reaching out to citizens[2] (variable 2).

Most of the indicators for citizen participation (dimension IIa) are also on the higher side: in each of the six districts, priority projects are defined through direct voting (variable 4); participation is universal (variable 5); and specific commissions, called District Participatory Councils (*Consejos Participativos Distritales, CPD*), are elected in each district on a yearly basis (variable 6). Members of the CPD can voluntarily become part of the oversight and control monitoring team for the implementation of PB projects (variable 9). However, the projects approved are essentially at the level of the neighbourhood level (variable 7) and do not relate to budgetary decisions at city level; this variable therefore classifies as a minimum arrangement.

An interesting and important facet of the Rosario PB experiment is its mainstreaming of gender through a number of mechanisms: (i) gender parity in the councils; (ii) projects with a clear gender perspective such as the prevention of domestic gender violence, awareness raising on sexual rights, strengthening of women networks, etc.[3]; (iii) the organisation of a "*ludoteca*" (childcare for babies and children) during meetings to facilitate the participation of mothers in debates; (iv) systematic campaign against the use of words and attitudes disrespectful of women. However, the only 'properly' actor-based aspect of the Rosario PB started in 2004 with the Youth Participatory Budgeting and 1%.

---

1 This represents approximately 1.5 % of total municipal budget and 22 % of municipal budget for investment (Rosario Municipality, 2012:12, Report for GOLD Report, unpublished material).
2 The unit developed a glossary of the basic terms used in PB, as well as game strategies to enliven the voting process (see J. Lerner's (forthcoming) 'Making Democracy Fun' based on the Rosario example).
3 From 2003 to 2011, 100 out of a total of 1200 approved projects were dedicated to projects with a clear gender perspective.

Table 2

of the PB budget has been earmarked for the Youth (Variable 8). For this variable, the Rosario PB has gradually evolved from a minimal to an intermediate arrangement and is heading towards a maximum arrangement with significant resources earmarked for the excluded. In 2013, the city introduced a voting system in Braille and translated the PB manual in one indigenous language, becoming the first city in Argentina claiming a multi-cultural approach to planning, spearheaded by PB.

As far as local government participation is concerned (Dimension II b), Rosario is doing well. Out of the 1200 projects approved since 2003, 900 have been fully implemented so far and the others are in the pipeline. This positions Rosario on the higher side on variable 11 (degree of completion of approved projects within two years).

Finally, from a normative and legal point of view (dimension III), the PB process in Rosario is regulated by an internal set of rules defined by the municipality and bylaws voted in 2002, subsequently modified in 2005 and 2006. These, however, leave some degree of leeway for each of the six districts councils (CPD) to shape the PB process including, for instance, in setting up venues and dates of the plenaries (variable 13). In terms of the relationship between PB and other planning instruments (variable 15), Rosario has been particularly successful in establishing a clear and functioning connection between decisions taken through the PB process and its Strategic Plan. In fact, many of the projects and priorities decided (and funded) through PB reflect decisions reached in deliberative processes in the context of elaborating the city's Strategic Plan. The very high score on this last indicator sets the Rosario case apart: PB, from the outset, has been seen as an instrument to bring about and enhance democratic decision-making in the Argentinian city, through democratic prioritisation of public resources.[4]

The grid thus provides important clues for assessing the extent and nature of a particular PB. Rosario's very high score on many of the analytical variables in the grid denotes a strong political commitment to the process. In turn, this reflects the particular emergence and rationale of PB in the Argentinian city of one million inhabitants. Participatory budgeting

---

4 The General Secretary of the municipality, along with the city's six Municipal Districts General Directorates, are in charge of coordinating the PB. The Planning Team of the General Secretary hosts the PB team and gives technical, intellectual and operational back-up to the whole process.

DIMENSIONS & VARIABLES ARRANGMENTS >	MIN	MED	MAX
I. FINANCIAL AND FISCAL DIMENSIONS			
1. Amount of debated resources		X	
2. Municipal budget allocation for functioning of PB			X
3. Discussion of taxation policies	X		
II. PARTICIPATORY (CITIZENS)			
4. Instance of final budget approval			X
5. Forms of participation			X
6. Which body makes budgetary priority decisions?			X
7. Community participation or citizen participation	X		
8. Degree of participation of the excluded		X	
9. Oversight and control of execution			X
II. PARTICIPATORY (LOCAL GOVERNMENT)			
10. Degree of information sharing and dissemination		X	
11. Degree of completion of approved projects (within 2 years)			X
12. Role of legislative branch	X		
III. NORMATIVE AND LEGAL			
13. Degree of institutionalization		X	
14. Instrumental or participatory logic		X	
15. Relationship with planning instruments			XX
IV. PHYSICAL / TERRITORIAL / SPATIAL			
16. Degree of intra-municipal decentralization		X	
17. Degree of inclusion of rural areas		X	
18. Degree of reversion of territorial priorities			X

Table 2 Rosario Participatory Budgeting profile *Source: Multi-variable Participatory Profile Method (MVPB), Cabannes, 2011, Belo Horizonte*

PB District Council meeting. © Courtesy of Silvio Moriconi

in Rosario arose out of a process of strategic planning initiated in 1996, in a context of administrative de-concentration of services and strong decentralization. However, the context of its adoption highlights a commitment to deepened societal governance associated with a political ambition towards more participatory democracy. For indeed, PB was effectively selected during a public consultation exercise in Rosario in 2001, as the best – most democratic – mean of tackling the municipal budget. The adoption of PB in Rosario, at the heart of the profound political and economic crisis that hit Argentina in the early 2000s, reflects the city's idiosyncratic radical tradition - and speaks to Rosario's on going dialogue with cities of similar character in the sub-region: Porto Alegre (Brazil) and Montevideo (Uruguay).

The reading of Rosario's PB experiment through the grid highlights the tool's analytical credentials. Specifically, it serves to highlight the differing underlying logics underpinning PB processes.

...sive Participatory Budgeting process in Rosario where efforts are made to assist blind people in participating and voting. ...urtesy of Silvio Moriconi

References

FORD, A. 2009. **El Presupuesto Participativo en Rosario, Una apuesta renovada al experimentalismo democrático**, Secretaria General, Municipalidad de Rosario, 58 pp, Proyecto Urbal, Red 9

Municipalidad de Rosario. 2011a. **Presupuesto Participativo: El trabajo en los Consejos Participativos de Distrito.** 18p.

Municipalidad de Rosario, 2011b. **Reglamento Interno del Presupuesto Participativo,** 4p.

UN-HABITAT. 2004. **Participatory Budgeting: Conceptual Framework and Analysis of its Contribution to Urban Governance and the Millennium Development Goals.** Concept Paper. Working Paper 140. July 2004. Nairobi.

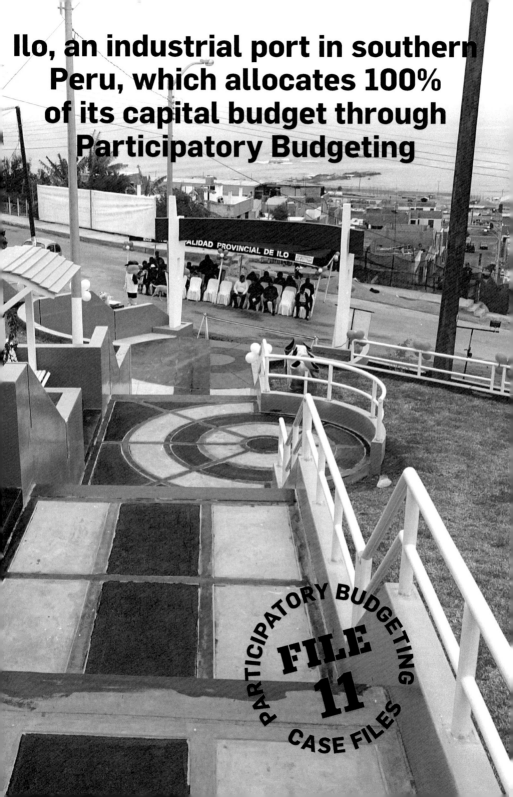

Ilo, an industrial port in southern Peru, which allocates 100% of its capital budget through Participatory Budgeting

Ilo, an industrial port in southern Peru, which allocates 100% of its capital budget through PB

Authors
Cabannes, Yves
ycabanes@mac.com
Delgado, Cecília
cmndelgado@gmail.com

Date
March 2014

Acknowledgements
This presentation was enriched by the work of and exchanges with various participants who have contributed to the participatory budget in Ilo since 2000, and in particular, Mario Villavicencio Ramirez, María Lourdes Blanco Mercado and Julio Diaz Palacios.

Website
www.mpi.gob.pe/
participacionciudadana/
cc.html.

Vídeos
www.youtube.com/
watch?v=XgpTrK9RfXY

Ilo, a unique city in the field of participatory budgeting

Ilo, the capital city of the province of the same name, located at the extreme southern end of Peru close to the borders of Chile and Bolivia, was the first Peruvian city to implement a participatory budget, back in 1999, one year before Villa el Salvador in metropolitan Lima. This mining port with a population of 63,000 people has maintained a record for longevity: the process has remained in place year after year, despite political changes in governmental administrations, making it important to understand how it has survived, when many times these changes mean the end to many budgets, even the most innovative ones. This issue will be addressed in brief 17, *volatility and the consolidation of participatory budgets*.

Another unique aspect is that the experience of Ilo was the point of reference for the design of the first National Law which, beginning in 2003, mandated every municipality in the country, and then each province, to implement participatory budgeting (see essential bibliography, brief 21). It was the former mayor of Ilo who lobbied for this National Law in the parliament, together with the Ministry of Economy and Finance from the executive side. A number of the protagonists of the Ilo budget, including the former Mayor, created a support, training and evaluation unit out of that experience, to help expand participatory budgeting in the country once it was mandated by law.

132

scale basic services network funded through PB. © Courtesy of Ilo Municipality

Origins: a tradition of participation and a struggle over environmental issues in one of the most polluted cities in the country.

The participatory budget of Ilo was not inspired by the experience of Porto Alegre, but rather by the long years of participation and environmental struggles which had marked the city from the 1980s. As Jose Luis Lopez Follegatti recalls (1999, Blanco-Mercado, 2007): *"one of the most important features in Ilo's development over the last 15 years has been the community management committees set up by residents, who have joined forces to carry out projects that directly benefit the community, such as paving streets, developing parks and installing water and electricity systems [...] Between 1990 and 1998, approximately 300 of these committees were created, each responsible for a project, with a total investment of about US$ 10 million".*

133

It is important to remember that in the 80's and 90's, Ilo was considered to be one of the most polluted cities in Peru, and represented a serious risk to its inhabitants. Years before the 1992 Earth Summit in Rio, Julio Diaz Palacios, before he became mayor, wrote a book entitled "The city we want", which provided a new vision of the city. Once elected, he turned to participatory budgeting, in which environmental protection issues are key. In a natural process, after the Rio Summit of 1992, the city endorsed the principles of Agenda 21, with a strong component of participation and multi-stakeholder management, in which the copper industry, the fish meal industry and residents are all considered to be part of the solution. A survey cited by Follegati (1999) found that "in Ilo, 67% of the population said that they had participated in a management committee [there were 300 committees in total], and 90% said that they had taken part or participated in some type of social, trade or cultural organization." It is out of this very socially fertile ground that the participatory budget emerges and grows, as will be described below (see the bibliographic references for more information).

Ilo, a mining town whose financial situation is unique among cities with participatory budgeting

As a mining city, and a main center of copper smelting in Peru, Ilo receives exceptionally large transfers from the central government, in the form of mining royalties. In this way, it is similar to other mining cities who receive the benefits of royalties paid by national or translational companies to national governments. Therefore, when taking regular budgetary resources and mining royalties together, Ilo is a wealthy city in Latin American terms, with a budget of 58.4 million dollars (152.86 million Peruvian soles) in 2012, equivalent to $2,388 per capita, more than double that of Porto Alegre and more than 300 times that of the Comuna VI of Yaounde, which is presented in this series. Another characteristic of the city which sets it apart is the very high proportion of the budget invested in comparison to current expenditures.

Ilo is one of the few cities which puts 100% of its capital (investment) budget up for debate through the participatory budgeting process. When it began in 2000, only 15% was debated; in 2001 this percentage rose to 40%, and was gradually increased until reaching 100% in 2007, which has

.y elected Oversight committee taking publicly their new role © Courtesy of Ilo municipality

been maintained to date. It is a good illustrative example of how a process can progressively be adjusted until the 100% level is reached. In 2012, participants discussed and voted on $13.3 million dollars, while in 2013 the number was slightly lower, $11.9 million, which gives us $211 dollars per resident in 2012, and $189 per resident in 2013, which are the highest numbers found anywhere to date in Latin America. They explain to a large extent the surprising and positive results obtained over the past 15 years. The exceptional transfers received by oil or mining towns are supposedly intended to compensate or ameliorate the exceptional environmental and social damages that they suffer. It is interesting to note that other cities have built their participatory budget with these resources; for example the case of Ampasy Nahampoana in Madagascar, which like Ilo has achieved significant results.

Participatory Budget in ILO		
YEAR 1 · Planning	**YEAR 2 · Execution**	**YEAR 3-10 · Maintenance**
PHASE 1 Preparation Preliminary steps Plan / timeline Awareness-raising / outreach Convening Registration Training **PHASE 2 Consensus-Building** Opening workshop and RC District and Provincial assessment and planning workshops **PHASE 3 Coordination** Technical-financial evaluation Meeting with technical teams Prepare proposed budget **PHASE 4 Formalization** Central workshop Final workshop	**TECHNICAL PHASE** Prepare technical dossiers Schedule work Select construction supervisors Request resources **SOCIAL PHASE** Coordinate with community Sign agreement First stone Execute project Inauguration Liquidate and close project	Plan maintenance Prepare file Execute Close

Stages of the participatory budget in Ilo *Source: Mario Villavicencio Ramirez, 2011*

Who participates: a representative community democracy

The number of people participating per year is surprising when compared to the thousands of participants in the Brazilian experiences, for example: from 108 in 2000, the number of participants has grown steadily and stabilized at around 4000 in 2010, 2011, and 2012. It is not the general public who participates, but rather delegates from "territorial" or neighborhood organization from the three districts that make up the Ilo province, as well as grass-roots, economic, urban, environmental and other organizations accepted in the process by authorities, and representatives of the various entities which by decree comprise the spaces of participation and governance, which will be presented below.

A strongly institutionalized process

One of the original facets of the Ilo Participatory Budget, and Peruvian processes in general, is that they are highly institutionalized, with precise structures and rules that are established not only in National Law 28056 and its regulations, but also in seven municipal ordinances, the last of which was enacted in 2010 (ordinance 479-2010 of 12/23/2010). These ordinances have been transformed over time. With its 20 pages and 56 articles, it defines the rules of the game, and makes them fully transparent. Together they codify a "community" pillar alongside the executive, legislative and judiciary branches. Despite possible limitations on the organizations that can participate and take part in this community power, it is an innovation in the area of local power that could explain how the process endures beyond the changes in administrations.

Forums for consensus-building and autonomous spaces for civil society

- The **Local Provincial Coordination Council (CCLP)** is a space for political-social consensus-building, comprised of authorities (mayors and councilors) and local representatives. The primary function of these councils is to guide the consensual planning process, and they are the final decision-making body of the participatory budget. The organizations are represented by one man, one woman, and since 2009, by one young person under 29.
- The first space for civil society is the **Participatory Budget Steering Committee (MDPP)**, which is comprised of six members elected from among the approximately 400 participating agents. Its primary function is to monitor the process.
- The second civil society forum is the **Participatory Budget Oversight Committee (CCVP)**, which is made up of six representatives chosen from among participating agents. Committee members are elected for two years, and their main function is to ensure the fulfillment of the agreements and commitments made during the process.
- There is also a **Permanent Participatory Budgeting Commission**, made up of 13 people: (i) the Provincial Mayor of Ilo and the two Mayors of the two other districts that make up the province; (ii) Three provincial council members and three civil society representatives who belong to the Local Provincial Coordination Council (CCLP); (iii) two members of the Steering Committee (MDPP) and (iv) two representatives from the Oversight Committee (CVPP).

137

Inauguration of PB project, Ilo. © Courtesy of Ilo Municipality

- The **neighborhood boards (12 in total)** are the grassroots organizations of the planning and budgeting process, who are grouped into **zonal assemblies** in each of the three areas of the Ilo District: Cercado, Pueblos Jovenes and Pampa Inalambrica.
- The **Works management committees** are social grassroots organizations in charge of supporting and supervising the execution of participatory budget-approved works and other projects. Members are selected by the neighborhood boards. (Villavicencio-Ramírez, 2012a)

The Ilo Participatory Budget is based on values and principles which gives it an ethical foundation, beyond its operational and financial aspects: participation, tolerance, solidarity, equality of opportunities, coherence, democracy, representation, efficacy and efficiency, competitiveness, co-responsibility, transparency and respect for agreements.

Priority given to basic services and infrastructure
The explicit priorities at the local level are first water and sanitation, second

road infrastructure, and third facilities. From a thematic perspective, the highest priorities are health and education.

Between 2000 and 2012, 665 projects were prioritized, and the vast majority of those have been implemented. One of the clearest results of the process is that potable water coverage in Ilo today is 96.3%, while sewer coverage is 87% (Mario Villavicencio Ramirez and the municipal technical team, 2012). One recent innovation that will be taken up again in the book on recommendations refers to *"financing actions according to the changes that they will bring about to benefit of the population, particularly the poorest [PB by results]."*

Highlights and shadows surrounding participatory budgeting in Ilo

We have selected here some of the highlights and shadows noted by M. Villavicencio Ramirez (Villavicencio-Ramírez, 2012b)[1]:

Highlights

- The participation of civil society through their representatives in the design of the regulatory framework, the planning, the outreach and the awareness-raising around the participatory process.
- The sustainable development approach is firmly rooted, with respect for the environment and for future generations.
- The quality of the participation of citizens is the result of a process of nearly 30 years, and the investment of resources in capacity-building efforts by the local government, NGOs and the civil society.
- The evaluation of our participatory processes in 2006 and 2007 helped us to assess how much progress we had made in relation to our Development Plan, what mistakes we had made, and finally to re-launch our participatory process. A new evaluation will be done in 2012.

Shadows

- Serious neglect of medium and long-term planning. The current perspective is very short-sighted.
- On the one hand, "authorities do not believe in participatory budgeting," and on the other, there is "confusion among some authorities who think that the Participatory Budget process is merely a formality of protocol, in

FILE 11 · ILO, PERU

---

1 These were updated in January 2014 (in an Exchange of correspondence with the authors)

which there is merely an inauguration and then a closing ceremony."
- The thinking that the process is the responsibility of only one area of the municipality, rather than accepting it as an institutional process in which everyone participates and contributes."
- There has not been any national evaluation of the process for over 7 years, which could help to introduce innovations. The Ministry of Economy and Finance, which is the lead institution in the process, has been silent since 2006.

These highlights could illuminate other processes contained in this book, while in turn other experiences could offer ideas on how to combat the shadows.

References

BLANCO-MERCADO, M. L. **Construyendo Desarrollo Democratico, Descentralizado y Sostenible.** Séminaire Démocratiser Radicalement la Démocratie, 2007.

LÓPEZ-FOLLEGATTI, J. L. 1999. **Ilo: a city in transformation.** LOCAL AGENDA 21. Environment&Urbanization Vol 11 No 2 181-202.

Municipalidad Provincial de Ilo - **Alcadia 2010. Ordinance N.º 479 - 2010** - MPI.

VILLAVICENCIO-RAMÍREZ, M. 2012a. **Guía para el Análisis de Casos de Presupuesto Participativo.** Internal Document.

VILLAVICENCIO-RAMÍREZ, M. 2012b. **La experiencia de presupuesto participativo en Ilo - Luces y Sombras de una gestión concertada para el desarrollo.** IV Seminario Internacional Presupuestos participativos 2012 - Democracia Participativa y Movimientos Sociales en Chile y América Latina actual.

PARTICIPATORY BUDGETING
FILE 12
CASE FILES

Seville, at one time one of the most advanced European PB experiences, unfortunately interrupted

Seville, at one time one of the most advanced European Participatory Budgeting experiences, unfortunately interrupted

Author
Cabannes, Yves
ycabanes@mac.com

Date
March 2014

Acknowledgements
I would like to express my gratitude to Virginia Barbarussa who has contributed her firsthand knowledge from the early days of the process and clarified some crucial points. My gratitude as well to Vicente Barragán and his colleagues from Pablo Olavide University for sharing the results of their unique research on the process.

Contacts
Seville PB [currently interrupted]
Vicente Barrágan,
participativos@gmail.com

Seville, with a just over 700,000 inhabitants (National Statistics Institute (INE), 2010) is the fourth largest city in Spain in terms of population. Its Metropolitan Area encompasses 46 municipalities, and is home to 1.5 million people (INE, 2010). The Participatory Budget in Seville began in 2004, and since then it has been an annual process. The victory in 2011 of a right wing party (*Partido Popular*) over the socio-democrat and leftist coalition that had launched the PB resulted in an interruption of the process, and raises the issue of how to address discontinuity, and beyond that, how to avoid these interruptions which usually result in the loss of the institutional and social memory of the experience.

Seville was the first large city and regional capital in Europe to adopt the PB, and benefitted from previous experiences in Spanish Andalucía. It quickly became a point of reference in terms of quality and innovation, which we will briefly highlight. Seville is clearly a spatially-based process, with a strong emphasis on the participation of children and youth. From a financial and fiscal viewpoint, just as is the case with Rosario, the municipal funding allocated to the implementation of the PB is relatively large, which made it possible to contract with various local universities and NGOs, especially in the earlier years. The technical support of an NGO, IEPALA, and the monitoring and research tasks taken on by local universities played an important part. Results from

the research and evaluation efforts were brought back to the stakeholders, and were used to fine tune the instruments, rules of the game [*auto-reglamentos*] and tools employed – in a nutshell, this technical support increased the quality of the whole process and helped to disseminate the experience throughout Spain and beyond. From 2005 to 2009, 70 million Euros were spent (or executed) to implement hundreds of projects, which comes out to an average of 14 million Euros per year. This amount that was put up for discussion each year varied from 2.6 to 3.7 % of what is called locally the "non bound" municipal budget[1]. In international terms (Cabannes, 2003), at approximately 25 to 30 American dollars equivalent per capita per year being actually spent for the PB, Seville ranks fairly high in terms of PB allocation.

Citizens' decisions in assemblies are final

Participation in the process is universal and open to all citizens. The rules clearly establish that the decisions made by voting in the citizen assemblies are binding, and the Local Government is mandated to implement them. Additional procedures were put into place to guarantee respect for the decisions made through the assembly-based direct democracy process. The first of these procedures is that the Local Government has to be transparent about how much public funding is available, and what it can be used for. The second is that oversight and control of project implementation, as in Porto Alegre and Rosario, are in the hands of "monitoring commissions", the members of which are elected during the assemblies to discuss project proposals. The research conducted by Vicente Barragán and his colleagues indicates that during the seven annual cycles, from 2003 to 2009, the number of hours of participation was close to 185 000, an outstanding indicator that demonstrates the interest of citizens in participatory budgeting[2]. The table below indicates the annual variation: during the 4th cycle, in 2007, the number of hours of participation jumped from 25586 to 39503, and despite its decrease in 2008 and 2009, it remained well above 30 000 hours per year.

An outstanding number illustrated by table 2 is the extremely high number of proposals made by people participating. Interestingly this number has

---

1 Barragán, V and all, op cit. 2011
2 Barragán, Vicente, Romero, Rafael and Sanz, José Manuel, op cit. 2011

PB Year	2003	2004	2005	2006	2007	2008	2009	Total
1st Round	2293	9348	5195	8338	10840	7433	5440	48885
CPD	6630	13620	11250	13080	15870	16290	16800	**93540**
2nd Round	914	1943	3305	4169	12794	10247	8984	**42353**
TOTAL	9836	24910	19750	25586	39503	33969	31224	**184778**

Table 1: Number of hours of participation at each step of participatory cycle [estimate]
Source: Barragán, Vicente, Romero, Rafael and Sanz, José Manuel, op cit. 2011

PB Cycle	2004-05	2005-06	2006-07	2007-08	2008-09	2009-10	TOTAL
Proposals	2091	2013	2230	2170	2778	3295	14577

Table 2: Number of proposals presented by PB participants
Source: Barragán, Vicente, Romero, Rafael and Sanz, José Manuel, op cit. 2011

been increasing during the last cycles, from 2170 for 2007-2008, up to 3295 for 2009-2010. In total, close to 15 000 proposals were made during the 6 years analysed that clearly shows that PB triggers people's capacity imagination and capacity to think the future they want.

Another unique feature of the PB in Seville is how smaller projects focused on the neighborhood / district scale co-exist with larger, citywide projects. The *"carril bicy"* (bicycle lane) was emblematic of the shift form community/ neighborhood based participation to citizen-based participation, with a project implemented at the city scale that dramatically changed the mobility of low-income residents, and their access to places of work or education.

People can decide on the rules of the participatory budgeting game. The role of the *"Comisión de autoreglamento"*.

Another salient and innovative feature of the process is its degree of institutionalization. While the process is formally established and enjoys a high degree of legitimacy, at the same time it is "self-regulated" in that the rules of the process are established and amended by the people themselves, primarily through the "Self-Regulation Commission" (*Comisión de Autoreglamento*) composed of elected delegates. The quality of the PB manual, which is regularly revised and enriched through a participatory process, has made it into a benchmark in the participatory budgeting field in Europe, and even beyond[3]. Interestingly enough, this rulebook, which guides the allocation of 15 to 25 million Euros per year of public money, has been taken to the city council on two occasions, and both times it met with virtually no opposition: all parties represented voted in favor, whereas the Popular Party (right wing) abstained, despite the harsh campaign against participatory budgeting led by the local newspaper (ABC) which is associated with the Popular Party. This clearly illustrates how the PB in Seville has been embraced by the legislature.

Below are some additional insights offered in October 2011 by Virginia Guttierez Barbarussa, one of the people responsible for the participatory budget, in response to a series of questions about some aspects of the experience.

How is the execution of the work controlled? A new sphere of civic oversight.

There are City Monitoring Commissions (who oversee the implementation of the proposals for medium-size works and activities), and District Monitoring Commissions (at the district level – small-scale infrastructure works and activities). The commissions meet periodically with the people responsible for the institutions, who report on what has been done, and how the money has been spent. If there is any problem in the implementation, or if a budget modification needs to be made, then approval is needed from 2/3 of the delegates to the Commission, along with the signature of the Citizen Participation delegate. This is codified in the rules of the Municipal Budget, which is annually approved by the full City Council. The commissions are made up of delegates elected in the assemblies.

The participatory budget deepens decentralization through the process of de-concentrating municipal services.

Were there about the same number of meetings as the number of Districts in the city, or were there more?

The Self-Regulations provides for 21 zones, and there are 11 districts; in other words, there are districts which can contain more than one. 3 open assemblies were held per year in each zone.

---

3 Autoreglamento de los presupuestos participativos.

A city wide bike lane was funded through PB. Seville PB was not limited to projects at neighborhood level. One of the m approved proposal was a city wide bike lane. © Courtesy of Seville Municipality

- The first was in October (to close the current process and launch the next year's), with three objectives: (i) to report on what was approved, and what was going to be included in the municipal budget, in case there was some modification or challenge to be made by the Assembly; (ii) to report on the implementation in progress and (iii) to choose the delegates to the Self-Regulation commission.

- The second meeting was in January or February, to report on what had been included in the municipal budget, to again report on the execution of the previous budget, and to review and approve the changes in the Self-Regulations.

- The third assembly, in May-June, was to discuss proposals. At this gathering, the project proposals are defended and voted on, and the delegates to the City and District Councils are elected. The Councils have two functions: in the first phase, after visiting the sites of the proposed projects and hearing from their proponents, they have to assess the proposals using social justice-related criteria. Once the projects are selected and prioritized (based on the voting and the application of the criteria), and incorporated into the municipal budget for the following year, these delegates then move on to form the Monitoring Commission, as described in the first point.

Are the Proposal Forums for deliberations only, or for making decisions?
The proposal forums are spaces for discussions, in which the "steering groups" (groups of volunteer citizens leading the process from the grassroots level), proponents and institutional representatives come together to discuss viability, adapt proposals to the legal framework and vice versa, join similar proposals, and to arrive at collective strategies to conduct the assemblies. But they are not decision-making forums. They are spaces for deliberation and co-management.

Beyond the steering groups, is there a "Participatory Budgeting Commission", or a similar entity comprised of elected delegates?
There are the City and District Councils, which later become the Monitoring Commissions. Their members are elected during the proposal assemblies.

Limits and reflections on the Seville process

- The first limitation is that despite the quality of the participatory budget in Seville, it was not able to withstand the political changes at City Hall, and today it no longer exists. What would have been necessary to minimize the risk of interruption? Was it even possible? These are issues that deserve special attention. From the beginning, the process in Seville was led by the *Izquierda Unida* party, a minority party in coalition with the Socialist Party. The process was not internalized enough within he local government and the population to continue on.
- Furthermore, there was no type of coordination between the participatory budget and the city's various strategic, local development or physical plans.

References

BARRAGÁN, Vicente; ROMERO, Rafael; SANZ, José Manuel, **Informe sobre los Presupuestos Participativos en la ciudad de Sevilla**, 2004-2009. Calidad democrática en los Presupuestos Participativos del ayuntamiento de Sevilla, Ayuntamiento de Sevilla. Universidad Pablo Olavide, March 2011, Final research report (in Spanish), 263 pages.

BARRAGÁN, Vicente; ROMERO, Rafael; SANZ, José Manuel, (unpublished research report), **Análisis del impacto de los presupuestos participativos en su capacidad transformadora,** Proyecto PARLOCAL, 2011. 106 pp.

Municipalidad de Sevilla, **Autoreglamentos de Presupuestos Participativos** (for each year)

BARBARRUSA, Virginia Guttierez, **En busca de una nueva cultura política. Los Presupuestos Participativos como Oportunidad.** Algo está pasando en Europa. V Jornadas Internacionales de Presupuestos Participativos, Sevilla noviembre de 2007. ISBN: 978 84 89743 54 0. Delegación de Participación Ciudadana Ayuntamiento de Sevilla-IEPALA. Sevilla. 2008.

BARBARRUSA, Virginia Guttierez, **La pedagogía de la decisión. La Pedagogía de la Decisión.** Aportaciones teóricas y prácticas a la construcción de las Democracias Participativas. Construyendo Ciudadanía / 10. págs. 131 – 144. ISBN 13 978 84 611 2443 5.Delegación de Participación Ciudadana – CIMAS. Sevilla. 2006.

A noteworthy experience in the 6th District (Commune) of Yaoundé, Cameroon: democratising and improving living conditions

A noteworthy experience in the 6th District (Commune) of Yaoundé, Cameroon: democratising and improving living conditions

Yaoundé's experience has been related in many documents, presentations, papers and evaluations published by ASSOAL for Local Development and the National Residents' Network, some of which are mentioned as references, namely, Achille Noupeou and Jules Dumas Nguebou to whom we express our gratitude. It also includes results of evaluation workshops conducted with one of the authors and discussions and correspondence spanning ten years.

Authors
Cabannes, Yves
ycabanes@mac.com
Delgado, Cecília
cmndelgado@gmail.com

Website
www.assoal.org

2003. Yaoundé 6 among PB pioneers.

December 2003 represented a milestone for Participatory budgeting in Cameroon. At the *Africités* Summit, a letter of intent, the culmination of months of discussions and debates, was signed by five communes in Cameroon, including Yaoundé 6, the Brazilian Municipality Cooperation Agency represented by the city of Caixas do Sul, the municipality of Montevideo, UN-Habitat's Urban Management Programme for Latin America and the Caribbean, United Cities and Local Governments Africa (UCLGA), ASSOAL for Local Development, a Non-Governmental Organisation from Cameroon, and the National Network of Inhabitants of Cameroon. Ten years later, in 2013, more than 50 cities in Cameroon are committed to this new approach of democratic management of public city resources, making Cameroon one of the beacons in Africa. Not only has the local government of Yaoundé 6 paved the way for PB, it has admirably maintained its focus, and strengthened a process that has been in operation every year from 2004 to 2013.

Some reasons to explain the strengthening of the process

The consolidation and the expansion of the PB process can be explained by three factors: the first is the decentralisation process and the 18/1/96 law that makes provisions for Decentralised Local Authorities within the Constitution. This paved the way for the 2009 Law on Budget Provisions (Nguebou

Neighborhood assembly in Commune 6, Yaoundé © Courtesy of ASSOAL

and Noupeou, 2013). The second factor, just as important if not more so, is the role played by organised Civil Society and, in particular, by the National Network of Inhabitants of Cameroon whose members not only seek to promote and increase the use of participatory budgeting, but are also responsible for ensuring that people play a leading role throughout the process. This commitment prevents the process from being used for political or technocratic purposes, as occurs in many cases. The third element that explains the continuity and efficacy of PB in Yaoundé 6 is the advisory and technical support offered by *ASSOAL for Local Development* and its close partnership with a local government that is open to and fully supportive of the new process.

Participatory budgeting with practically no budgetary resources: what is the scope and value?

The very limited budget is one of the primary challenges faced by the local government of Yaoundé 6 and its 268,000 residents (Noupeou et al., 2012).

PB workshop at neighborhood level: analysis of potential projects. Commune 6, Yaoundé. © Courtesy of ASSOAL

It is a challenge shared with other communes in Cameroon, and more generally, the vast majority of African local governments. The annual budget per inhabitant is more than 100 times smaller than the budget per inhabitant in a city such as Porto Alegre! The total municipal budget in 2009 and 2010 was less than $ 6 per inhabitant, and the amount allocated through participatory budgeting was less than $ 1 per inhabitant per year. That sum rose to CFA 51.7 million in 2012 and should have increased to CFA 75.5 million by 2013 (Noupeou, 2011). Although these amounts are small, approximately $100,000 to $150,000 per year, they are vital given the serious challenges that Yaoundé and the Commune face, with high levels of unemployment, particularly among young people, with 40% of its inhabitants living below the poverty line, and with very limited social services and poor water supply.

The first lesson from this experience is clear and simple: the PB model implemented – we will describe the most salient and innovative features below – is all the more significant because resources are limited.

152

One important feature of this case is that the resources discussed and allocated through participatory budgeting are almost twice as much as those allocated by the Yaoundé 6 local government. One of the joint initiatives conducted by the various stakeholders is to raise extra budgetary resources, for example, through international cooperation with the European Union. Dondo, Mozambique (see file on Dondo in this book) is another example of a local government that demonstrated its capacity to mobilise international resources, for projects decided by people.

The second lesson that can be drawn from this case is that because citizens' monitoring systems have been set up to monitor accounts, the resources allocated are certain to be used for projects that lead to tangible improvements in the life of residents. This also avoids the risk of corruption or mismanagement that often eats away at limited resources. The control and monitoring system is in line with a wider citizens' monitoring and oversight program that enables residents to react to events through text messages, sent free of charge using a hotline number (8033), or to report on progress made on projects being carried out in their districts (ASSOAL, 2012).

The third lesson is that, "the tax recovery rate and taxes overall have increased and this has led to a rise in tax revenues" (Noupeaou, 2011). Tax revenues increased by 6% between 2009 and 2010, and by 10% between 2010 and 2011, which is quite significant[1] (Noupeou et al. 2012). This increase in revenue allows for greater funding from locally developed resources of the projects committed by the local government.

However, the main reason for starting a participatory budgeting process in a commune with severe poverty and very limited budgetary resources is that PB serves as a redistribution mechanism enabling, from both social and spatial perspectives, greater access to basic social services considered critical for the population in any given area. Some of the projects approved in recent years allow for detailed measurement of the contribution made by participatory budgeting to better living conditions: Maintenance and rehabilitation of secondary roads; improving access to drinking water; expansion of the electric power grid and public lighting network; installing street lights; access to health care; the building of 23 standpipes; and the management of drainage gullets, open drain cleaning, and water piping.

---

1 Calculations were done by the authors based on information provided by Achille Noupeou, Bertrand Talla Takam, Daniel Nonze, Jules Dumas Nguebou, Achille Atanga and MayorAdjessa Melingui (GOLD questionnaire, 2012)

Pathways funded through PB in low income neighborhood. Community participation allows to make more with limited fu conquered through PB © Courtesy of ASSOAL

Two clearly defined cycles: budgetary programming and identification of priorities by the people in Year 1 (Cycle 1) and project implementation in Year 2 (Cycle 2).

Yaoundé 6 was one of the 'laboratories' where the method and the different stages of each cycle were tested and documented[2]. It currently takes the following steps: (i) creating the budget for the commune and determining priorities; (ii) meeting of the participatory budgeting coordination committee; (iii) setting up the basic social services observatory; (iv) Monitoring preparatory activities and calls to tender; (v) Monitoring launch sites; (vi) Monitoring and evaluation of work being conducted; (vii) monitoring ceremonies for approval of work completed; (viii) Evaluation and presentation of progress reports.

Three significant innovations

The Participatory Budgeting Council: an original governance model for African cities, and not only for Yaoundé 6.

The City Council remains the body that makes the final decisions on the city budget. However a new multi-actor entity, known as the **Participatory Budgeting Council** is in charge of selecting the final projects and engaging in discussions with the Executive branch. The PB Council meets twice per year and is chaired by the Mayor. It is made up of representatives from the Commune's Executive branch, the private sector and civil society. Two representatives are elected by each of the 24 neighbourhoods in the Commune – 48 in total – from among residents who are both dynamic and interested in managing local affairs. One of the responsibilities of these representatives is to manage the budget and monitor the projects undertaken. They organise meetings, with the people in charge of the Observatory of Basic Social Services, to inform the executive branch about the progress of project being implemented and are therefore the link between municipal authorities and residents. Some confidence between the residents and the local government seems to have been restored. However it is highly dependent on the districts representatives who play a role of intermediaries, and ease out tensions between both sides.

---

2 For more information, see Cameroon Alliance for Participatory Budgeting and Local Finance - Alliance Camerounaise du Budget Participative et de la Finance Locale, 2010

Wealth and employment creation

The projects that receive the majority of the votes in the PB Council are those allowing access to basic social services, considered critical. However an innovative element for participatory budgeting in Yaoundé, which can be attributed to the efforts of ASSOAL for Local Development and the National Residents' Network, is the inclusion of projects that enable wealth and job creation, especially in the informal sector, as eligible for funding. This step forward is all the more important given that more than 90% of the economy of Yaoundé is informal and that there are no clear policies to develop that economy.

Information Communication Technologies – ICTs – keeping residents informed and democratising the process

One of the major innovations to participatory budgeting introduced in recent years and underscored by the Cameroon Alliance for Participatory Budgeting and Local Finance (Alliance Camerounaise du Budget Participatif et de la Finance Locale, 2013) is the use of text messages and mobile phones to keep the population informed and to invite people to become involved in the process:

Residents are kept informed about the process with text messages on the activities being carried out by the Office of the Mayor with the ICT4GOV programmes. "Participate in forums and make decisions!" For example, on January 31, 2012, a text message was sent by the Executive of the 6th Commune of Yaoundé to 25,000 residents to inform them about the budget to be allocated to priority projects voted on in the 2013 Participatory Budgeting Forums and to encourage them to participate in the citizens' debate by voicing their opinions and by attending the district forums starting August 4 in 23 districts in the area. Just after this message was sent, another was sent to invite residents to the various upcoming forums. A reminder was sent on the day before the event to each resident to let them know where the forum would be held in their area. An example of the message sent to residents in Mendong neighbourhood: "Participatory Budgeting Forum in Mendong, August 4, 2012, 9:00 am at the Chefferie. Contact: SM. Mvondo Jean. Come out massively and decide which projects should be funded! Mr. Mayor"

juration of a paved pathways. Note that the resources to implement this PB project where mobilized through foreign
ntralized aid © Courtesy of ASSOAL

Future constraints and challenges

There are myriad constraints perceived by the primary stakeholders, despite
the extremely positive results obtained so far. In summary, these are:

- At central government level, there is no enthusiasm for this approach and
civil society participation is viewed with suspicion.

- At local government level, because there is no legal framework for
participatory budgeting, the process is dependent on political will and the
commitment of key officials. Some believe it is a tool for drumming up
votes from the electorate.

- Civil society organisations are often criticised because they are disorga-
nised and their functions are unclear

- The involvement of residents in the decision-making process is still limited and the participation of some groups such as those who live in slum areas, young people, and women is even more limited (adapted from Nguebou and Noupeaou, 2013).

Meeting these monumental challenges makes progress made in Yaoundé 6 neighbourhoods even more significant.

References

Alliance Camerounaise du Budget Participatif et de la Finance Locale. 2010. **Les étapes** [Online]. Available: ecolegouvernance.tmp38.haisoft.net/index.php?option=com_content&view=article&id=10&Itemid=34 2013].

Alliance Camerounaise du Budget Participatif et de la Finance Locale. 2013. **Africités 2012: BP et TIC étaient à l'ordre du jour** [Online]. L'école de la Gouvernance au Cameroun. Available: ecolegouvernance. tmp38.haisoft.net/index.php?option=com_content&view=article&id=2 61:Africités-2012-BP-et-TIC-étaient-à-l'ordre-du-jour&catid=31:budget-participatif-et-gouvernance-locale&Itemid=143 [Accessed 20/10/03 2013].

ASSOAL, P. L. D. L. 2012. **Yaoundé VI: A quand se tient l'Assemblée communale du BP?** [Online]. Available: www.assoal.org/index. php?option=com_content&task=view&id=451.

NGUEBOU, J. D. & NOUPEOU, A. 2013. **Experiência de Orçamento Participativo nos Camarões.** In: LOCO, A. I. (ed.) Esperança Democrática - 25 anos de Orçamentos Participativos no Mundo.

NOUPEOU, A. 2011. **Budget Participatifs en Afrique.** CGLU-A Fiche d`Expérience de BP - Commune d`arrondisement Yaounde 6. Cameroun. Document interne.

NOUPEOU, A., TAKAM, B. T., NONZE, D., NGUEBOU, J. D., ATANGA, A. & MELINGUI, A. 2012. **Guide pour L`analyse de cas du Budget Participatif.** Document interne.

Participatory Budgeting in secondary schools in the Nord-Pas-de-Calais Region, France

PB in secondary schools in the Nord-Pas-de-Calais Region, France

Authors
Cabannes, Yves
ycabanes@mac.com
Delgado, Cecília
cmndelgado@gmail.com

Date
2014

Website
www.nordpasdecalais.fr/
jcms/c_5220/le-budget-
participatif

Videos

Explications sur ce que finance
la Région dans les lycées:
www.nordpasdecalais.fr/
jcms/c_53123/zapping-videos/
budget-2013-explications-sur-
ce-que-finance-la-region-dans-
les-lycees

Le budget participatif des
lycées en action: www.youtube.
com/watch?v=l_1XgczKTRO

PB involving young people, children, school children and university students

Participatory budgeting involving young people began in 1997 in Barra Mansa, Rio de Janeiro, Brazil, and from there spread out appearing repeatedly, often spontaneously, across Latin America, Europe and North America (Cabannes, 2007). Expansion of Youth PB is quite different from standard PB, such as that developed in Porto Alegre, and the two processes often occur independently from one another. To understand the differences between the processes, one needs to examine and differentiate between the following typical situations:

Participatory budgeting involving *children* attending primary school, has occurred, for example, in Icapui, Brazil, with its "Happy Day" (Dia Feliz), and in Cotacachi, Ecuador, where children are invited to determine how part of the municipal budget should be spent. In some cases, such as in Cotacachi, and more recently in Seville, Spain, PB for young people is one component of a larger PB process. whereas in Barra Mansa, participatory budgeting for adults did not exist. Funded projects could focus on life at school (improving playgrounds, increasing the amount of time buses stop at bus stops to allow the youngest children to board the buses calmly or banning teachers from smoking in class…!) or on the city as a whole, for example, installing speed bumps in certain areas or paving sloping streets that are particularly slippery.

PARTICIPATORY BUDGETING
FILE
14
CASE FILES

160

Participatory budgeting also exists for *young people* also exists for both girls and boys of secondary school age, whether or not they attending school. Very often public schools, more so than private schools, are used as venues for holding meetings and debates. This occurs at São Bras de Alportel in Portugal and very often in Peru where participatory budgeting is practiced in all local governments. It also occurs in cities in Sweden, La Serena, Chile, and others in the United Kingdom. Like the category above, city resources are made available to either improve schools, their environment and equipment, the neighbourhood, or the wider city.

Participatory budgeting in primary and secondary schools. Public resources earmarked for primary and/or secondary school education will be discussed. At least two typical situations should be highlighted. In some countries, such as Brazil, education can be under the responsibility of the local government. Therefore resources for education are discussed are part of the municipal budget. This occurred in the city of São Paulo, Brazil, where several hundreds of thousands of euros (541 million Reales) earmarked for schools and literacy projects for young people and adults were discussed in 2001 and 2002. The second category of resources belong to organisations at the regional level, as in the case of participatory budgeting for secondary schools in the Nord-Pas-de-Calais Region, France, where the regional, and not central or municipal governments, is in charge of budgets for secondary schools.

Participatory budgeting at university level. For some years now, there has been a new type of participatory budgeting in some universities, private universities in particular. This is the case for instance in Argentina and Brazil, where part of the budget is made available to students so that they can suggest activities that would either improve the way the university operates, or allow local citizens access to the university, for example, by offering courses to people living in the city who may not have enough money to go to university or to become specialised in a particular field.

A region marred by poverty and inequality

The Nord-Pas-de-Calais Region (comprising approximately 4 million people in 2010), formerly a textile industry hub during the Industrial Revolution

Pauvreté et inégalités en France

La pauvreté par département

Inégalités de revenus par régions

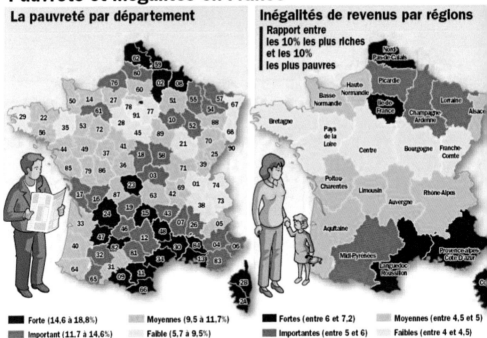

| Forte (14,6 à 18,8%) | Moyennes (9,5 à 11,7%) | Fortes (entre 6 et 7,2) | Moyennes (entre 4,5 et 5) |
| Important (11,7 à 14,6%) | Faible (5,7 à 9,5%) | Importantes (entre 5 et 6) | Faibles (entre 4 et 4,5) |

Poverty and inequality in France. The Map indicates that the Region Nord-Pas-de-Calais [top of the maps] suffer high poverty rates and extreme inequality. *Source: Observatoire des Inégalités*

and once upon a time ? the largest mining region in the country, is now marred by joblessness resulting from deindustrialisation exacerbated by the 2008 global financial crisis. *The poverty and inequality in France map – see maps 1 and 2 –* clearly show that it is one of the poorest regions of the country; between 14.6% and 18.8% of its population is poor. At the same time it belongs to a group of regions with the widest gap between the rich and the poor. At its core, Participatory Budgeting in Secondary Schools in the Nord-Pas-de-Calais region aims to foster a school system that promotes equality of opportunity, and that also gives school children confidence in democratic voting and in a political system that for many is only associated with negative circumstances in their day-to-day lives.

Some functions of the regional government developed just thirty years ago as part of the national decentralisation process, relate to the construction, operation and maintenance of secondary schools and vocational training centres. At the start of the 2013 academic year, 180,000 people were enrolled in 184 public secondary schools and 94 private schools, with a regional budget of €279 million. The budget for vocational training centres (23 000 people enrolled in 23 centres) stood at €142 million. (Nord-Pas-de-Calais Region, 2013).

A swift upscaling of a new process

Nord-Pas-de-Calais Region was inspired by a similar experience conducted between 2005 and 2012 in the Poitou-Charente Region where 1800 projects were voted on and the majority of them implemented. It should be noted, however, that the Nord-Pas-de-Calais Region introduced several innovative features to the process. It only began in 2010 as an experiment in five institutions each offering a different type of training (vocational secondary schools; 'urban' secondary schools and agricultural secondary schools) enabling the model to be very quickly adapted to each institution. Between 2011 and 2013, PB had been conducted in 25 secondary schools; the current aim is to reach all schools before 2015.

From a financial perspective, each school decides upon approximately €100,000, a rather large sum of money that political decision-makers justify by stating, "we do not want to encourage cosmetic participative democracy by asking secondary school students to just choose the colour of the wallpaper. This level of resources allows for genuine projects to improve quality of life or to support educational community initiatives" (Cau, 2013). Above all, these projects seek to improve the quality of life (for example by purchasing furniture for training centres or by installing water fountains) and to enhance existing facilities, for example, by refurbishing common rooms or boarding school showers (Charter, 2013).

The current PB cycle is spread over two academic years, and allows secondary school students to see the outcomes of the decisions they have made. The 2013/2014 PB cycle follows seven steps: (1) Commitment by the Board of Directors of the school and the setting up of a monitoring committee; (2) Meetings between the monitoring committee and regional authorities; (3) Joint project development and submission to the regional authorities between September and December 2013; (4) Examination of projects by the Region regarding feasibility and costs between December 2013 and March 2014; (5) Debates and voting on priority projects in schools from March to May 2014; (6) Vote confirmation by the regional authorities from July to October 2014 and finally (7) Project implementation by the regional authorities before the 2014-2015 academic year.

Once debates and deliberations have been completed, voting is conducted by the simple 'one person-one vote' principle and, generally, available resources enable two or three projects to be funded in each school every year. The Charter, a similar tool to the rules of procedure that exist for many of these processes, stipulates that:

"The aim is to reach the minimum threshold of 10% of the total student body of a school at the voting meeting. In addition, students must account for at least half of the voters. The remainder of the persons voting must cover all the following categories: teaching staff; administrative staff; technical and health staff and parents".

One of the results of this pluralist and original voting method is that the projects selected can benefit both the students and the technical staff. This occurred at the Sallaumines Vocational Secondary School, where the projects chosen for 2011-2013 included: (1) the building of a conference room, an archiving area and a common room for technical staff; (ii) making the playground more attractive and (iii) setting up a language laboratory [www.lp-sallaumines.fr].

A governance model based on the "educational community" concept and a multi-actor monitoring committee

One of the original elements of PB for secondary schools is its governance model. The Monitoring Committee is particularly interesting in several respects. It is made up of a maximum of 15 people; membership is not limited only to secondary school students, although they must have a majority (eight out of 15). The seven remaining members are teachers, administration and technical staff, parents or any other person affiliated with the school. The Participatory Budgeting Charter clearly stipulates that the gender mix should be respected and all groups should be represented. This monitoring committee drives the entire process and recalls the PB "Catalyst Groups" [*grupos dinamizadores*] from Seville, Spain. It shoulders many responsibilities and, in particular, *"it ensures that the PB process works smoothly with Directorates of the Regional Authorities; that the charter is respected and distributed to all members of the educational*

ipatory Budgeting in secondary schools. *Source: Video Explications sur ce que finance la Région dans les lycées*

community; that PB related issues are properly communicated; is involved in mobilising all stakeholders and their right to free speech and coordinates project delivery", (Charter, 2013). As a result, this committee provides a forum for debate and discussion among social groups who usually do not engage with one another or are in conflict. In this way, above and beyond the specific benefits of any projects funded, this diverse committee fosters the concept of an "educational community" put forward by regional political decision-makers. The committee avoids focusing the secondary school issues only through the participation of students but expands it to all concerned actors who have to learn to reach agreements.

Involving the Monitoring Committee all through the two-year process

Another interesting aspect is that the Committee is responsible for both Participatory Budgeting cycles: determining which projects should be priorities in Year 1 and monitoring the implementation of these projects in Year 2. In the last 25 years, experience has clearly shown that Year 2 cycle is just as important and perhaps even more than the first year one. It is during the second cycle that ideas become reality and decisions become tangible. In addition, a period of two years is sufficient time for committee

Participatory Budgeting in secondary schools. *Source: Video Explications sur ce que finance la Région dans les lycées*

members to learn to listen to each other, understand each other and engage in genuine dialogue.

In some cities, Monitoring Committees shoulder more responsibilities, for example, they may participate in openings and analyse tender offers. The committee in the Nord-Pas-de-Calais region also has important functions: *"It is involved in selecting equipment (if any): for example, model and colour in line with regional services standards and cost of the project voted on; it can challenge regional services regarding the scheduling of the work to be completed; it takes photographs of projects as they unfold: before, during and after; finally, it organises an event to celebrate the end of projects"* (Charter, 2013).

Improving the school environment above and beyond projects

One of the principles of the first set of secondary schools involved in the participatory budgeting process underscores that an important end-result has been achieved: "The school environment is much calmer. There has been a significant decline in the level of anti-social behaviour displayed; there is greater confidence among teachers and students who now feel as though they are playing a part in the changing school structure. There is more respect for the school, its equipment and for ancillary and management staff: they have had the opportunity to get to know each other better and share their points of view…!" (Morelli, 2013)

Scaling up and sustaining the process

A current challenge, noted by a number of stakeholders, is the difficulty of reaching all secondary schools in a short timeframe however we can consider this a predominantly human constraint rather than a financial one. One might very well wonder how disruption to the process, as occurred in Poitou Charente PB, could be prevented: can the existing multi-actor governance model provide continuity to a Participatory Budgeting process currently that is fiercely promoted by only one political party? This is a challenge for the future and for young people. The other challenge, of course, is understanding the extent to which this highly democratic process will challenge inequality in the Region and assist young people in finding jobs and good living conditions.

References

CABANNES, Y. (2007:4) **Des Budgets participatifs "jeunes" en Amérique latine,** ADELS, Paris

CAU, M. 2013. **Lycéens citoyens à vous de décider! Lancement du budget participatif des lycées.** Blog de Myriam Cau [Online]. Available: myriamcau.over-blog.com/article-lyceens-citoyens-a-vous-de-decider-lancement-du-budget-participatif-des-lycees-56778389.html 2013].

MORELLI, S. 2013. **La démocratie participative appliquée au budget des lycées.** La Voix-l'Etudiant.

Région Nord-Pas-De-Calais 2013a. **Charte du Budget Participatif des Lycées (BPL)** - 2013. www.nordpasdecalais.fr/upload/docs/application/pdf/2013-09/bpl_charte_2013.pdf

Région Nord-Pas-De-Calais 2013b. **Rentrée 2013-2014 dans les lycées du Nord-Pas de Calais.** Dossier de Presse.

Participatory Budgeting as a way to reducing the urban - rural divide in China: the Chengdu massive experiment

PARTICIPATORY BUDGETING

FILE

15

CASE FILES

Participatory budgeting as a way to reducing the urban – rural divide in China: the Chengdu massive experiment

This paper draws on a longer presentation available online eau.sagepub.com/content/early/2013/11/19/09562478135 09146 co-authored with Zhuang Ming, Chair of the Chinese NGO Huizhui Participation Centre and that was updated in October 2013 with joint field visits, as part of UKNA [Urban Knowledge Network Asia] research on "Cities by and for people".

Authors
Cabannes, Yves
ycabanes@mac.com

Date
March 2014

PB in rural areas are numerous, often innovative but scarcely critically documented

Documentation and critical information remains quite scarce on participatory budgeting processes taking place in villages or in small rural settlements, despite their variety and high number primarily in Africa and in Latin America. Some of these processes take place some times only in the rural districts of larger cities, for instance in Cuenca, Ecuador where no PB exist in the urban area. Sometimes they occur in rural local authorities and in all hamlets and small villages that are part of them, as in Fissel in Senegal. Chengdu, the fourth city in size in China is quite unique as participatory budgeting was massively introduced first in rural peri-urban villages and localities as a way to reduce the economic and social gaps that exist between the urbanized areas and the peri-urban and rural hinterland. Before introducing the experience, lessons learned and limits, a few challenges shared by Chengdu, the Capital of Sichuan, along with most Chinese cities allow to better measure the relevance and uniqueness of the case.

Urban – Rural divide, democratic aspirations and collec-tive & individual land rights: three major challenges for Chinese metropolis, including Chengdu.

Participatory budgeting is very much embedded in a set of reforms initiated by Chengdu municipal

government from 2007 onwards to respond to some particular concerns. In fact, participatory budgeting has to be viewed against the backdrop of three major challenges in Chengdu that are common to most cities in China facing booming economic growth:

(i) *Rural–urban divide.* Despite economic growth, even when villages are close to rich urban areas they still have incomes and levels of services that are inferior to those in urban areas; the per capita income of an urban family was 2.63 times higher than that of a rural family in Chengdu in 2007. Moreover this did not change in Chengdu between 2003 and 2007, despite extraordinary economic growth;

(ii) The second challenge refers to commune autonomy and villagers' rights and their aspirations to local democracy; and

(iii) The third relates to collective land use rights of villagers and security of tenure, both for housing and for agriculture, which are seriously under threat as urban areas expand.

Eligible projects or loans

Participatory budgeting in Chengdu started in 2009 and has continued ever since. At present, it is the largest in China in terms of the number of projects funded and the amount of resources allocated, as discussed below. Projects eligible for Participatory budgeting are primarily "... *public services that can be delivered and monitored by local villagers and residents.*" (Chengdu Municipality, 2008) These fall into four major categories: (i) culture, literacy and fitness: which includes village radio and cable, TV, village library, entertainment and fitness; (ii) basic services and infrastructure for local economic development: including village roads, drainage, gardening, irrigation and water supply; the projects selected or voted on in this category represent more than 90 per cent of the funding; (iii) agricultural training, such as farming and business training for villagers; and (iv) village management, which includes village security and village administration; sanitation and solid waste collection fall into this category and not under "basic services" as in most countries.

In addition, villages can apply for a loan along with the Participatory budgeting funds they receive, to allow them to finance larger projects. The maximum loan they can get from Chengdu Small Town Investment Company (public) is seven times the amount of the Participatory budgeting

Training programs for villagers by village PB funds. © Courtesy of villagers

resources that have been allocated to a project. This is very helpful when some costly Participatory budgeting projects are prioritized, such as a village road.

A significant budget amount to be discussed and decided upon

Chengdu Municipality and its township governments set aside budgets for rural public services. One of the major strategies applied by its *Commission for Balanced Rural and Urban Development* was the improvement of rural public services through the Village Public Services and Public Social Administration Reform. Over the three PB cycles during the 2009–2011 period, the total value of projects funded in Chengdu through the PB process was equivalent to around US$ 325 million and the annual amount is increasing gradually year-on-year. If one considers that the rural population is five million people, the amount per villager per year to implement PB is around US$ 22, quite a high figure when compared to other renowned PB experiments (Cabannes, 2013) The amount allocated to each village rose in 2012 and varied between US$ 40,000 and US$

80,000 (250,000–500,000 RMB). The variation depended on a limited set of criteria such as remoteness and level of public services.

An original model of governance with village councils at the core of the process

Since its inception, PB has been the responsibility of *village councils* elected in each one of the 2308 villages around Chengdu where the process is taking place. . . In addition, the budget oversight group within the village councils, which consists of five to seven elected local villagers, monitors and oversees the implementation of the budget. This is a clear innovation within the Chinese budgetary system, which increases the capacity of villagers to control the spending of public money. In the villages of Chengdu, direct democracy is practiced regarding PB – an open villagers assembly makes the final decision, while the village council can be viewed as the standing committee.

PB cycle in Chengdu

PB cycles are not identical in all localities. Most commonly, villagers go through a three-step cycle in order to identify, select and implement their public services projects. The first step is that village council members gather proposals from all village households as to what projects they need. In various villages, each household receives a standard printed form to fill in with what they would like to be funded. The second step is decision-making by those elected to the village council, who vote for the projects that will be implemented in the coming year. The third step is monitoring during the implementation of the project with a key role played by the oversight group, composed of village councilors or other innovative governance models designed locally.

Main differences with the rest of participatory budgeting in China

(i) An endogenous process.

It was largely designed with limited reference to international experience whilst other experiences in China are internationally supported or led, and it may be more difficult to sustain them as their process has not been located from the outset within the local political and administrative structures.

(ii) An innovative policy and not a mere program

This means more institutionalization and a set of pre-established rules, but at the same time it also ensures more stability. Interviews and meeting with politicians responsible for PB revealed how much it was embedded as a tool for reducing the rural–urban divide. It also has considerable potential for expansion both in Chengdu and in other Chinese cities.

(iii) Massive scale for a participatory budgeting process.

It is not taking place in one village or in a limited set of villages or rural communities but in all 2,308, and it is reaching five million rural people in Chengdu. Now that it has been expanded, even if modestly to the urban districts as well, its outreach is a city of 11 millions registered people. Most PB experiences in China, including the most innovative ones, are essentially exclusively urban based and quite limited in scale. They are mostly consultative and are usually not fully open to the general public, or are limited to public hearings. The level of resources planned for 2013 is in the range of 264 millions euros for both urban and rural areas of Chengdu city and possibly the largest one at world wide level, even if still a drop of water in Chinese standards.

Some contributions of Chengdu participatory budgeting worldwide

Support to productive projects

One of the debates over the last 25 years of PB is whether participatory budgeting should finance productive and income making projects or not. Main argument against is that public money should not be for the benefit of individual interests. As a result, very few cities have included these types of projects in their list of eligible projects. In Chengdu, infrastructure for economic development is one of the villagers' central priorities and at the same time is fully accepted by municipal and township authorities. This includes paving roads which will facilitate the marketing of fresh food and livestock, and the maintenance of water channels and riverbanks that are part of the irrigation networks that have underpinned farming in this region for centuries. The rationale is that these projects should be a means to develop the value of the land still a collective, and therefore not in contradiction with public resources that would benefit individual interests.

...ers voting for village PB funds projects; each household has one vote. © Courtesy of villagers

Ultimately participatory budgeting is conceived as policy tool to reduce the social and economic gap between urban and rural areas of Chengdu metropolitan area. Evidence gathered in 2013 in some villages clearly suggests that rural roads have helped local productive and commercial activities to flourish such as pig stalls close to the road or forestry related activities.

Food – Land – Participatory Budgeting nexus
One central idea of this first book from the collection **"Another city is possible! Alternatives to the city as a commodity"** is that in some parts of the world innovative approaches led by communities start to connect one with the other and have a powerful leverage effect. Chengdu is a good example of such connections and nexus. Collective forms of tenure

Villages sports games funded by village PB funds. © Courtesy of villagers

on arable land associated with participatory budgeting and with food production are reaching remarkable effects on improving quality of life and living conditions of villagers. The powerful impact of such connections would need to be further investigated and quantified.

Key concerns and challenges for the future of participatory budgeting in Chengdu

Expand PB from village to township level and from rural to urban.
One year ago, in 2012, we identified this expansion as a major challenge. In effect, PB was possible in Chengdu's villages because villages are relatively autonomous. However, as suburban villages become urbanized, and are administered as urban districts, this could be a threat to PB. The control of the Chinese Communist Party is stronger in townships and urban districts, which are key to economic development. Interestingly enough, since then participatory budgeting has expanded to urban consolidated

districts, even if at a more modest scale than in villages. Visits in September 2013 evidenced the acceptance of the approach by the authorities and the existence of elected community councils in the urban areas, equivalent to the village councils in rural areas that are the movers of the participatory budgeting dynamics. One can wander what their future will be.

Participatory Budgeting generates a citizen's divide

Chengdu counts about 6 millions people living in urban districts, 5 millions in urban areas and 3 millions people who have been registered to stay for more than six months (*Hukou* registration system). If one includes those who are not formally registered as residential households (and therefore not entitled to some public services), the population can be estimated at between 15 and 18 million. One of the limits of participatory Budgeting so far is that project proposals and ballots are limited to "native *Hukou*". As noted in villages visited in 2013, registered migrants and the floating population of non-registered people, therefore the most vulnerable and that in some settlements can be half the population, are not entitled to participate to date. One could argue that they benefit from the projects voted for instance in the case of street paving or greening alleys. However, they are not participating citizens and PB draws a social dividing line with newcomers.

References

CABANNES, Yves (2014) **Contribution of Participatory Budgeting to provision and management of basic services. Municipal practices and evidence from the field** IIED Working paper, downloadable at pubs.iied. org/10713IIED.html

CABANNES Yves and ZHUANG Ming (2013), **Participatory budgeting at scale and bridging the rural–urban divide in Chengdu,** Environment and Urbanization, published online 19 November 2013. Available: eau. sagepub.com/content/early/2013/11/19/0956247813509146

Chengdu Municipality Administration Office (2008), **Document No 38.**

Participatory Budgeting in Paris:
Act, Reflect, Grow

PARTICIPATORY BUDGETING

FILE

16

CASE FILES

Participatory Budgeting in Paris: Act, Reflect, Grow

Authors
Cabannes, Yves
ycabanes@mac.com

Date
April 2017

Acknowledgements
We express our gratitude to the
Paris municipality and primarily
to the Vice-Mayor's Office
for Local Democracy, Citizen
Participation, Associativism and
Employment, and to its PB staff
[Mission Budget Participatif] for
their support and for providing
detailed and unpublished
information. This chapter would
not have been possible without
their contributions. All figure
and information contained in
the chapter, unless otherwise
mentioned, is official data
available on PB site or from the
city itself.

Website [French]
https://budgetparticipatif.paris.
fr/bp/le-budget-participatif-.
html

Credits ©, to be inserted under
each picture
Courtesy Mairie de Paris

File Cover Picture
2014 approved project, part of
a series of works of art on blind
façades. Commissioned artist
Fabio Rietim © Courtesy
Mairie de Paris

1. Paris, a rising star in a bright PB sky

Over the past years, various global and capital cities such as Madrid, Seoul, Delhi, Taipei, Bogota, New York or Paris have started quite significant PB processes or expanded them upon much more radical basis (see file 1). Paris is one of these latecomers and already shines as a rising star in a PB bright firmament. It is worth unpacking the experience from various angles, but primarily because of the clear demonstration at the core of this book, that PB is conducive to trigger and expand radical alternatives, for instance in urban agriculture, arts and culture and to avoid evictions and house more decently vulnerable people such as homeless, refugees or migrants. At the same time, PB appears as a bridge, or glue between these various alternatives, and help them to shift from an isolated innovative field into a much more powerful system that addresses critical dimensions of our urban day-to day life. Even if each PB in these capital and global cities brings cutting edge elements and are innovative in their own rights, Paris remains remarkable on budgetary an participation issues when compared with its sisters.

le driven mobile poll boxes, located in strategic public spaces in order to encourage voting. © Courtesy Mairie de Paris

Important budget per inhabitant put into debate. The quantity of resources Paris (2.3 millions inhabitants) is allocating for PB reached 100 million euros in 2016, after a gradual increase during the first two cycles, in 2014 and 1015. Interestingly, Madrid, another newcomer is allocating the same amount for its own PB. However, when comparing the amount debated per habitant per year, simply dividing the amount debated in a specific year – in US $- by the number of inhabitants, Paris ranks first in this group: PB investment per inhabitant per year is close to ten times more than what is being debated in New York [about US $ 35 millions for 8.6 millions inhabitants] or in Seoul [about US $ 46 millions for a population over 10 millions]. Less than 5 US $ are debated in these two cities, and around 50 US$/Inh. for Paris. Madrid with its 100 millions € for 3.2 millions inhabitants [2016] amounts 36 US$ / inh and is getting close to Paris. Even if the numbers rank Paris or Madrid in the top end when compared

181

Public presentation and vote for 2016 PB projects. © Courtesy Mairie de Paris

with most experiences, a broader worldwide analysis [Cabannes, 2015] indicates that some smaller or intermediate cities are debating much more resources per inhabitants. A recent case is São Bernardo do Campo, inserted in the Metropolitan Region of São Paulo and the fourth Brazilian city in investment capacities: PB debates per inhabitants over 3 times what is debated in Paris or Madrid (145 US $ in 2015 and 2016 despite a plummeting exchange rate between Brazilian Real and US dollar). The amount debated <u>and spent</u> in absolute numbers amounted 221 millions US$ for bi-annual cycle 2015-2016.

One original and positive aspect of Paris PB was to announce an overall PB value of 500 millions euros for the whole 2014-2020 mandate. This is relatively uncommon, but quite innovative as it raises a sense of medium term perspective and helps build confidence between the city and its citizens. They realize that these resources are quite significant and that PB is a key tool, even if still limited [5 % of total investment] when compared with Paris overall budget amounting close to 10 billions euros. At the same time, opening up a secured medium term perspective allows citizens and grassroots to develop their own strategies and proposals through time. Among the rare cases where a multi-annual perspective was introduced,

Chengdu (see file 15) emerges as a unique case, as villagers can either choose to spend PB resources on immediate actions or use it as a down payment for taking a collective loan for much larger projects. PB allocation over the next years, with a maximum of seven years, will repay this loan. Fortaleza in Brazil pioneered a PB that discussed in the first year of the mandate the overall financial budgetary envelope, and then each following year debated the earmarked annual budget. However, the reference case remains São Bernardo do Campo, mentioned in the previous section, that designed and developed during 8 years corresponding to two municipal mandates a unique multi-annual PB, called PPA [Plano Pluri Annual] that translates Multi Annual Plan [Consórcio Intermunicipal Grande ABC, 2013].

Significant level of participation. Just as important as the B [budgetary leg] of PB is the P [or its participatory leg]. It will be analysed in more details later on in this chapter, but once again justifies to have selected Paris. The level of participation in the city has grown significantly [from 40 000 voters in 2014 to 92 809 in 2016 that represent 5% of the total population. When adding the participants in the PB in schools the number of voters jumps to 159000. These figures are much higher than in other capitals. However, proportionally, participation can still grow and remains modest when compared with some PB champions. For instance in Cascais, Portugal, (see file 6 in the present book), an intermediate city of 206 000 inhabitants [data 2012] located in Lisbon Metropolitan Region, 58567 people voted in 2016 [28.3 % of total population] for PB.

Over the next section on Paris PB specifics and original aspects, some salient aspects that make Paris experience remarkable will be organized around dimensions largely used to unpack PB at city level: [a] budgetary and financial; [b] Participatory that differentiates both citizen and government participations and [c] institutional and legal framework. Promising outcomes and results achieved are briefly highlighted in section 3, illustrated by examples of projects that demonstrate that *"another city is possible with PB".* Section 4 explores why this was possible in about 3 years that is quite a short period of time in PB standards.

2. Specifics on Paris PB and original aspects

Various PBs are flourishing in Paris, gradually enriching the process.

MAIRIE DE PARIS

VOUS AVEZ VOTÉ
PARIS L'A FAIT

BUDGET PARTICIPATIF ///////////////////////////////////
BILAN DES ÉDITIONS 2014 / 2015 /////////////////////////
Mise à jour en septembre 2016

You voted, Paris implemented it. Participatory Budgeting

Over the 3 last years, various types of PB have been gradually added and this mushrooming experience covers four different processes that fall under the PB umbrella:

[a] A Paris wide PB that debated 30 millions euros in 2016 for projects for the City as a whole

[b] Twenty PB processes carried out in each one of the 20 districts [called *arrondissements*] that are part of Paris. It is to be noted that each one of the *arrondissement* elects its own Mayor and its councillors. They will elect a Mayor for Paris as a whole. These twenty PB are relatively independent, despite flowing the same charter [Ville de Paris, PB Charter, 2016] and are spearheaded by the district/*arondissement* staff. They debated 64.3 millions euros in 2016, with significant variations from one district to the other. Interesting to note that Madrid is following a similar pattern, with 30 millions euros for projects at the scale of Madrid as a whole and 70 millions for projects in each one of the 21 districts.

[c] PB for working class neighbourhoods was introduced in 2016 in order to transfer resources to the most needy. Again the 30 millions euros at stake are divided up half and half, into city and district scales.

[d] Youth and schools PB taking place in all public schools, at primary, college and *lycées* level.

In 2017, some spin-offs agreements are made with RATP, the public society for transport in order to expand PB to this company that is essential for commuters and Parisians all the same. Another agreement is under discussion with Low income Housing Management Companies and could lead to new PB processes, not discussing municipal budget but institutional ones. An interesting precedent in capital cities, among quite a limited number, has been taking place over the last 15 years in Toronto, where Toronto Community Housing debated with tenants around 5 millions Canadian dollars in 2016, with $4.23 million for general capital items including common spaces, and $750 thousand for safety projects.

Basic data on PB financial and budgetary dimensions

Over 500 millions euros are earmarked for PB to be debated over the 6 years of the mandate stretching from 2014 to 2020. This amount is all the more significant as in 2016, Paris is transferring the significant amount of 500 millions euros out of its income to other French cities and regions, as part of the national equity policy. At the same time, Paris is one of the few large French cities that have not increased local taxes. At the same time since 2013 and up to 2016, transfers from central government have decreased by 41 % from 1291 millions euros down to 774 millions. As a result, PB resources had to be found within flattened budgetary resources and clearly points out the political willingness that was necessary to earmark 500 millions euros for PB.

PB and Public Participation

A permanent PB team of 9 people conducts the day-to-day activities and is part of the Vice-Mayor office for local democracy, citizen participation, associativism and employment. This limited staff connects with 50 focal points within a huge city of Paris administration of over 50 000 employees. Because of its high political linkage and its careful administrative design, PB has been able to permeate the whole administrative machinery. For instance, around 300 civil servants [internal resources] are involved in the feasibility study stage with a strong back IT office managed by the permanent staff.

In order to keep an internal coherence and mobilization, a *steering committee* composed of high-level representatives from PB concerned directorates within Paris administration such as finance or citizen's participation meets every fortnight. They will review each one of the projects proposed by individuals or citizens' organizations that are organized under thematic entries. As a result of this collegial discussion, the projects will be either instructed by a specific directorate or simply rejected. Four eligibility criteria help to accept or reject a proposal: [1] need to be proposed a Parisian, meaning a resident; [2] satisfy general interest; [3] be part of the city responsibility; [4] running costs of the investments related to projects need to be limited and primarily should not imply generating a public job. These criteria for PB are still decided by the city as part of the PB charter and not by citizens as for instance in Seville or in Brazilian cities where the PB Council meets every year and adjust the PB rules and criteria.

...shop for co-construction of projects, gathering different individuals and associations who proposed similar projects or ...ts that could develop in synergy. © Courtesy Mairie de Paris

Citizens' participation in some key steps of PB cycle: project selection and final voting

Citizen's role in Parisian Commission for project selection. Decision-making for PB project selection that will be further voted by citizens appears a key moment in the whole process. Specific commissions exist in each of the 20 districts. In addition, a *Parisian Commission* selects Projects at City scale. Different from most council and forum from Latin America that are essentially composed of delegates selected by participants, the decision making commissions in Paris, either at district or city scale levels are mixed public/citizens outfits with a short majority of civil society representatives. The Parisian Commission is composed of 9 members from the executive and legislative branches of Paris Government: [1] The Vice Mayor for local democracy, citizen participation, associativism, youth and employment; [2] First adjunct in charge of culture, heritage, trades of art, cultural and night enterprises and relations with districts local governments; [3] Vice Mayor in charge of finance, public/private economy enterprises, public biddings and concessions; [4] A representative from each political group part of Paris City Council.

The Citizens counterpart is composed of 10 members: [8] eight people are selected randomly from Parisians registered on the PB web platform: 2 out of citizens that presented individual projects; 2 out of those that presented projects as a collective; 2 out of those that presented a project as Neighbourhoods Councils; 2 out of citizens that registered on the web platform; [1] A representative of the Parisian Youth Council and [1] A representative of the Council of Students from Paris.

This mixed council is particularly interesting as it gathers high ranking city members and gives space to various collectives that have been directly involved in PB, and therefore gives continuity and learn from past

Street located PB poll box © Courtesy Mairie de Paris

accumulated experience from committed citizens. At the same time it connects with the 122 Neighbourhood Committees widely spread in the various districts and probably the main channel for participation at local level in the city. The engagement of representatives from the Youth and students echoes the willingness to engage with youth and give continuity to PB in schools and colleges.

So far the commission has no responsibility on PB project implementation and fiscal control as in many of the experiences presented in this book. This might change in the future when PB project implementation will become a dominant activity.

Citizen's participation for final project selection: on line vs "physical" voting
One key moment in the Parisian PB cycle is final voting for projects that were screened by the city staff and subsequently selected by the commission we just described. All Parisians residents can vote, irrespective of age and nationalities, up to 10 projects located where they live or where they work Capital cities and more generally cities from the north are tempted to focus on voting though internet, despite the limited debates and face to face discussions that this system implies. Interestingly Paris has been promoting both on line and physical ballot: about 200 ballots boxes are located in different spots to ease out direct voting (see pictures). In addition 50 % of the ballot boxes are mobile, drawn by bicycles and held in public spaces such as squares, schools, market places. As a result of this effort towards "physical " voting, the proportion of on-line votes curved down from 62 % of total in 2015 to 49 % in 2016. More importantly, given the increase of numbers of voters in absolute terms, the number of "presential" voters [Chris, need help on presential] jumped up over the two years.

A remarkable aspect of PB in Paris lays in its capacities to trigger the imagination and the creativity of both individuals and civil society organisations: they proposed around 3200 projects in 2016 and 2600 in 2017, according to preliminary results. These projects usually under a draft form, once reviewed and selected by the municipal commission previously mentioned, will become potential projects and each one of them is visible on line on the PB platform [PB Paris web site]. The persons and organisations that proposed similar or complementary projects are invited to meet and participate in "co-construction" workshops that are normally ending with much stronger programmes with different projects, or sub-projects. This explains why a very high number of proposals end up into a much reduced number of eligible cluster of projects: the 3200 proposed projects in 2016, once clustered into larger proposals ended up into 219. One of the benefits of this process, largely supported by the permanent staff, is that isolated projects, usually located in a specific neighbourhood will gain a critical mass and become citywide. The example of the "Home for Homeless" program that was ranked first in 2016 will be explained further ahead.

Legal framework and institutionalization of process

A *BP Charter* adopted by Paris Council [https://budgetparticipatif.paris. fr/bp/le-budget-participatif-.html] highlights the key aspects for people to be informed and participate: who can propose a project; how can you participate; which are the eligible projects; what is the selection process; how voting takes place; calendar of key dates; follow up of project implementation and mapping of projects, etc. Unfortunately, the Charter is still formulated by the local government, even if debates are taking place to open the possibility of citizens' consultation to modify, as in most countries, the rules of the PB game.

A strength of Paris PB that might explain its swift expansion and mushrooming through time is to connect with a broader and already established Participation System. PB is only one among various participation tools, but relatively well connected to them. Other mechanisms connected to PB are summarized below:

– *Citizen's councils* [neighbourhood councils, citizen's conferences, Paris Youth Council, Council for the Night, Council for Paris students,

– Citizen's map / *La carte citoyenne*, that opens possibilities to participate to training sessions on public engagement or to meeting councillors

– Multiple digital tools such as *Epetition* a platform to launch a petition, or *I commit,* that facilitate linking up Parisians with grassroots and organisations looking for volunteers.

– *Collaborative actions and projects:* re-invent Paris, call for projects for instance on Urban Agriculture and farming *[Paris'Culteurs],* citizen's conference on social housing or climate

– *Capacity Building and Training*: workshops for citizens, permanent university for elderly and retired, etc.

Past research results suggests that PB experiences that are able to connect

Voted PB Project: Ideas Box for solutions for Refugee Centre. © Courtesy Mairie de Paris

with other forms of participation are among the most sustainable through time if and when they avoid draining people's mobilization from the whole system and emptying these other participation channels from their social energy. It is a risk as today PB with its exceptionally high budget in relation to other forms of participation might mobilise citizens, at the expense of other forms. It does not mean, at any point in time to reduce PB amount, but much more to increase resources earmarked for other forms of participation.

3. Highlights on results and some innovative voted projects

This section aims at summarizing the evolution of key aspects of Paris PB and more importantly to highlight the type of projects that are actually voted. The central argument is that over three years the proportion of projects heading towards another possible city and the reclaiming of the Right to the city is quickly expanding.

It started in **2014** when nine projects out of 15 proposed by the city only where voted by 40745 citizens. Summing up a budget of 17 millions euros, their implementation started in 2015. The examples below, for the city as

Urban farming in schools. Project approved in 2014 and currently running © Courtesy Mairie de Paris

whole clearly indicate that the programs selected and voted [called projects in Paris] cluster numerous projects [called locally sub-projects]:
[a] network of 14 co-working spaces for students- entrepreneurs [2 millions euros]; [b] 40 vertical gardens to cover "blind façades" all through the city [2 millions];
[c] Street arts by local artists and grafters with a 3 millions € budget (see pictures);
[d] Kits for "pedagogical gardens" for 212 schools [1 million €]

In **2015**, out of 5000 projects submitted either by individuals [2/3 of total] or collective [1/3], 1500 qualified as feasible and 8 projects were selected by 70000 voters for Paris as a whole, and 180 for projects at a district scale. The budget at stake exploded in relation to 2014: the 8 projects for Paris amounted 35.2 millions euros whereas the 180 district scale ones summed

Exemplary PB project under the voted *Homes for the Homeless vote program*: A derelict building is transformed into a centre for refugees and migrants. © Courtesy Mairie de Paris

up 37.7 millions. Even if PB is open to any sectors and issues, over 60% of projects concentrate on four sectors only: living environment [25 % of total]; environment [15%]; transport and mobility [13 %] and culture and art [8%]. Interestingly Innovative solidarity programs for vulnerable groups, primarily the homeless appeared and were selected[1]. Other selected programs contributing directly to the building of "another possible city" such as urban farming and no-cars alternative gained high visibility and significant resources. Among the 8 projects for Paris as a whole, the following can be highlighted as particularly innovative:

[a] Support and help to vulnerable people: shower and washing facilities for homeless and poor; left luggage spots with lockers, etc. [4.4 millions €]
[b] More bike lanes and equipment such as security, lockers [8 millions €, 14718 votes]

---

1 Twelve thematic entries in 2015: built environment; Culture and heritage; economy and job; youth and education; nature in the city; Cleanliness; living together; sport; transport and mobility; smart and digital city

Homelessness is a critical issue in Paris and Parisians expressed their solidarity with homeless, refugees and migrants: the program *Home for the homeless* was the most voted PB project in 2016. © Sophie Robinchon. Mairie de Paris

[c] Urban farming and urban agriculture: shared gardens, roof gardening, orchards, educational gardens [2.3 millions €]

In **2016**, the number of projects submitted decreased to 3160, out of which 1500 qualified as feasible. The number of voters continued to increase to 92 809. For the first time the scale of 100 000 millions euros of approved projects was practically achieved [94,4]. Three areas are of prime interest in relation to building another possible city grew in importance: Urban agriculture and greening the city; Arts and culture and more importantly **solidarity and social cohesion.** Four programs clustered numerous radical ideas for a non-commodified city, notably:

– Food, from wasting to sharing
– Solidarity with the homeless
– A citizen's space *["kiosque citoyen"]* in every low income neighbourhood
– Fostering civil society dynamics *[vitalité associative]* in low-income neighbourhoods.

194

Solidarity with the homeless: PB as a means to build another possible city.

Out of the 400 plus projects voted over the last 3 years, *Solidarity with the Homeless,* the first choice of Parisians in 2016 is probably one of the most innovative one, as it clearly indicates that PB can kick off solidarity and radical ideas to address homelessness as an unsolved problem in most cities, primarily large ones. It illustrates once again the idea that participation and PB are turning individuals into citizens able to prioritize humanitarian and right bases issues, instead of starting with projects that would selfishly benefit them, their family or their neighbors. It substantiates the hope that *another city is possible with participatory budgeting.*

The rationale for the program *"solidarity with the homeless"* is to increase the possibilities for the homeless to meet their needs and access basic services. The program aims as well to test new forms of individual or collective housing solutions and projects are clustered along four sub programs:
– 3000 survival and health kits to be distributed to homeless
– Call for projects for arquitects and planners to envision and design innovative spaces and forms for individual and collective solutions for temporary and/or mobile shelters
– Contribution to the setting up of a refuge shelter for migrants, that is a dramatic issue in Paris and in most European cities.
– Designing and creation of an app. listing in various languages practical information on resources to eat, wash, be cured, leave and lock ones' luggage, and emergency housing.

An invisible dimension of Paris PB that is worth unveiling are the original ideas that were proposed in the first instance, and that were subsequently scrutinized and selected or rejected by the local authority commission, and then developed and clustered into four projects and one program. They are the heart of the innovation, either coming from individuals or from grassroots and civil society organisations. They seem the true gold mine to build other possible cities. Selected originals projects that generated the final sub programmes illustrate this idea. They are squarely translated from French to keep their original concept:
– Shelter for people with no permanent address
– Habitable structure, Studio Lib, will propose security, comfort and hygiene, and will improve living conditions for those sleeping rough

PB voted project. Traditional and historic *"Bains Douches"* where Parisians can take showers and bath when their apartm not provided with the service, are now refurbished and improved for servicing homeless people. Here art deco Bains-Do building located in Oberkambf neighbourhood, © Courtesy Mairie de Paris

– Self built stable habitat for Parisian Romas people.

– *Eleft* luggage for homeless people: public hot spots to digitalise and store information on the net and/or USB flash drive for administrative and personnel data.

– Shelter for pavement dwellers

– An application for migrants designed with organizations working with them in order for instance to gather all information useful for them.

– Solidarity telephone: It looks like a telephone that can be fixed on a lamp post of bus stop that would attract people to facilitate meetings. Its main function is to tape messages and listen to them, and therefore maintain a conversation with anybody living in the street.

– Open space [public bath and shower / *bains douches*]: " I would like to see in *République* neighbourhood a social centre for Homeless and other people in need that would allow them to take a shower, wash their clothes and protect their effects.

Beyond the uneven quality of these drafts and their level of development what remains striking is how PB final proposals have been able to maintain the inventiveness and radicality of original ideas, expanding them instead of fading them down. As expressed by the local PB team, one of the major contribution of PB, and the condition for its survival and sustainability lies in its capacity to find out-of-the-box solutions, or at least feasible ones that a city administration could not have invented and put together.

the project under the *Homes for the homeless* voted PB project is to increase the level of investment for this recently built ᵉe centre. © Mairie de Paris

PB sparking off radical struggles and policies of citizen's initiative

An interesting offshoot of the PB program on Homes for the homeless came when two major Civil Society organizations LDH [Human Rights league] and MRAP [Movement Against Racism and for Friendship among People] addressed an open letter to Paris Mayor requesting immediate solutions for hundreds of homeless and for people leaving in slums [*bidonvilles*] and threatened with short term evictions. This letter sent in January 2017, i.e.

a couple of months after the program Homes for Homeless became the most voted in Paris, highlights the importance of PB " Financial resources do exist, as Parisians who expressed their solidarity positioned the PB project Homes for the Homeless as their first choice". PB is acquiring for movements not only a financial dimension but a policy and political ones. We argue here that PB can become a starting point for broader struggles and for the formulation of policies of people's initiative. This links back to the original definition coined in Porto Alegre (see file 2 in this book) when PB was not only a way to define the use of municipal resources but a political tool to have a direct impact and control over policies, Whether or not PB will have an impact on Paris policies remains to be seen but is worth following up.

4. Why such an expansion and positive outcomes were possible in such a short time?

· **A Clear political commitment and strong political will** from the Mayor and Paris senior decision makers: Since the very beginning, Anne Hidalgo, Mayor of Paris, boldly committed herself and her government for PB to be a success and turn change visible (see poster, *le changement ça se voit*). Her foreword transpires this engagement and her readiness to face potential political obstacles: *"Obviously, starting up such a project means to accept facing criticism, debates and challenging opinions. It means as well to engage into a totally transparent process with citizens. But we should neither fear debate [...] nor transparency, as it is under citizen's scrutiny that democracy prospers"*.

· **A significant amount of earmarked resources,** amounting 500 millions euros over the 2014-2020 mandate, allowed to mobilized citizens and most importantly various participation channels that were already existing in the city. It allowed as well spreading the process in Paris as a whole, but at the same time rooting it into the various districts, schools and colleges and low-income neighborhoods.

· **Learning by doing.** One challenge faced by this PB among many comes from it top down initiative. How to mobilize citizens remains a challenge,

Among many Paris dull and blind façade, Rue d'Aboukir. ©Patrick White
(http://www.verticalgardenpatrickblanc.com/node/4676)

primarily in Europe. In a country well known for its long and sometimes winding debates that sometimes are slowing the action, Paris took a radical opposite trend, relatively courageous and humble. PB started quite experimentally, shifting long reflections to immediate actions in a learning-by-doing perspective. **Act first, reflect and move up** became a motto that was and is permanently repeated, as one of the first PB coordinator expressed: *"Do and think instead of Thiiiiiiiiink and [maybe] do!"*. The approach is summarized along three guiding principles: *[a] Be **bold**. Start quickly. It won't be perfect right away, but strong forward momentum will contribute to collaboration and meaningful progress; [b] **Dynamic evolution**. Be ready to be flexible and open to change. Structure and administration might be modified through trial-and- error and [c] **Collaborative input**: Innovation can't happen in a vacuum. Provide tools for a dialogue between administrative teams and citizens to achieve an effective final product together* [Mairie de Paris, 2016].

Vertical garden transforming a blind façade into an urban oasis, rue d'Aboukir. Artist Patrick White. It inspired the PB pr
"Gardens on walls" voted in 2014 © Patrick White (http://www.verticalgardenpatrickblanc).

· Triggering citizens' imagination and desires

PB quality depends primarily on people's ideas, proposals and engagement. The swift expansion of participation and of proposed projects in all sectors of urban life probably lies in the appropriation of the process by citizen's themselves. PB probably filled an historical void and a backlog of small and large projects that matter for people. What is remarkable, and probably explains an important people's engagement in a city from the Global North, is the level of pedagogical tools and means that were designed and applied: guidelines on how to present a project; simple and accessible power points on know it all on real costs; interactive web platform for citizens to react, expand, add up and improve a proposal; numerous face to face and on line training workshops for emergence of ideas and projects formulation http://www.paris.fr/atelierscitoyens , Co-building workshops when proposals are on quite similar issues or located at the same place, web-based monitoring and mapping of project implementation. This echoes opinions regularly expressed in Brazil for instance by Pedro Pontual who was one of the main agent for Paulo Freire's educational movement and PB pioneer, *PB must be primarily a university of active citizenship* [Pontual, P, 2004, Era Urbana, see file 23 on must reads on PB]

· Mainstreaming PB within Paris huge administrative machine [modernization of the administrative system and working modes]

PB in Paris has dramatically changed public management methods at city level, at least in two directions: first the various directorates need to react and implement much more quickly in order to implement the projects that are voted in a much shorter time span when compared with conventional ones; the second is that most of the 400+ voted projects over the last three years require the involvement of more than one directorate and therefore internal cooperation between two or more services. The changes required to address these two challenges would not have been realized without the strong political leadership and will from the Mayor.

Another remarkable aspect is how PB permeated a huge and hierarchical administration employing about 50000 civil servants. The design as previously described allowed for mainstreaming both horizontally and vertically PB within the system:

– At horizontal level for instance, [a] PB *steering committee* composed of staff from key directorates meets every fortnight and helps for internal communication; [b] the inter-directorate selection sessions of eligible projects that concludes on whom should follow up each proposed project stimulates as well horizontal mainstreaming; the official appointment of 50 reference officers in the directorates complemented the in-house mainstreaming of PB.

– At vertical level, for instance, the permanent PB team of nine persons maintains regular contacts in each of the 20 districts with civil servants in charge of the various participation channels, such as the neighborhood councils.

PB as a way for reclaiming the Right to the city

One of Henri Lefebvre key contributions that led to framing the Right to the City theory was that day-to day life could be inductive to radical changes in the way to design and build cities [Lefebvre, *La Vie quotidienne dans le monde moderne*, 1968, Gallimard]. Parisians engaging in PB, contributing with their thousands of creative ideas in the different realm of the day to day life [vie quotidienne] perfectly illustrate Henri Lefebvre's insights and aspirations when he was writing that radical transformation will happen in cities, and not only in factories [as in the Marxist doxa] but through the transformation of our day to day life under its multiple forms. The choice of Paris to leave PB menu open to any aspect of quotidian life of Parisians and to implement creative proposals paves the way to reclaiming the Right to the city, precisely where Henri Lefebvre lived and struggled for it.

References

CABANNES, Yves, **Contribution of Participatory Budgeting to provision of basic services in cities**, Environment & Urbanization, 2015 International Institute for Environment and Development (IIED). Vol 27(1): 257–284

Consórcio Inter-municipal Grande ABC, **PPA Regional Participativo Grande ABC,** 2014 -2017, Decembre 2013, Santo André

LEFEBVRE, Henri **La Vie quotidienne dans le monde moderne,** 1968, Gallimard

HIDALGO, Anne, Mairie de Paris, **Participatory Budgeting in Paris goes digital,** 2016, power point, Tudigo & Bulb in Town, Paris

PONTUAL, Pedro, **Construyendo una pedagogía de gestión democrática: El Presupuesto Participativo como "escuela de ciudadanía"** , in Era Urbana, 2004, Edición especial sobre presupuestos participativos, Quito, Programa de Gestión Urbana

Ville de Paris, **Charte du Budget Participatif,** 2016

Part 3

ISSUE BRIEFS

The contribution of Participatory Budgeting to the democratisation of local governance

PARTICIPATORY BUDGETING

FILE

17

ISSUE BRIEFS

The contribution of Participatory Budgeting to the democratisation of local governance

Author
Cabannes, Yves
ycabanes@mac.com

Date
January 2014 [French]
August 2014 [English]

The main idea conveyed here and supported by several experiences related in this book is that participatory budgeting is conducive to creating new forms of governance:

Firstly, by encouraging new forms of community and citizens' organisations to emerge, through budgetary decision-making (Cycle 1 of PB) and implementation (Cycle 2). PB contributes to developing and strengthening a fourth branch of local democracy, i.e. the power held by citizens/communities which is linked to the other three branches of government – executive, legislative and judiciary. It forges innovative relations with the other three branches of government that would require greater analysis. Some experiences, among those that are more advanced, help to create forums where citizens can use their power and countervailing power.

Secondly, by creating new forums for discussion, and often, new decision-making bodies comprising of both local government and social organisations, thereby strengthening *"societal governance" that focuses upon the dynamics of relationships between public and civil society spheres.* These new spaces, that are more or less institutionalised, and which will be addressed in greater detail in this document, help to bring about a shift in power relations for the benefit of citizens, and at times, albeit rarely, for the benefit of more marginalised social groups.

1. Participatory budgeting sometimes encourages countervailing power from citizens/communities

An examination of the 12 PB experiences documented in this book qualifies and updates conclusions drawn from an analysis of 30 PB cases from across Latin America and Europe that took place from 2000 to 2003[1]. In the majority of cases, organisations made up entirely of citizens are created to lead, regulate and often to make final budget decisions. This situation occurs more frequently than it did ten years ago.

(i) Participatory Budgeting Councils as a reference model

Participatory Budgeting Councils, referred to as COP in Portuguese, remain a central reference point for citizen power, comprising of councillors elected from among representatives who were themselves elected in the various thematic and space based assemblies. The number of members, the ratio of women to men; the quotas, for example, to ensure there is representation from vulnerable social groups, the most marginalised groups (migrants living in certain cities, for example), or groups with a small number of members (the homeless community) will vary greatly from one city to the other. Nonetheless, in general, these "Councils" are made up only of elected citizens, both male and female, without representatives from the local government. This is the case, for instance, in the city of Guarulhos (PBC); Belo Horizonte (COMFORCAS) and Ilo in Peru with its "Participatory Budgeting Board". Seville has a City wide Council based on its "District Councils". These special councils are specifically created for and during the participatory budgeting process. They have different responsibilities and functions in each city, ranging from simple consultation to decision-making. Their mandate is renewed from time to time, usually every year or every two years, and their operating rules are modified and adjusted over time.

Alternatives to COPs When participatory budgeting is only "space based" and does not address specific sectors at the city level, these councils are made up of elected neighbourhoods representatives such as in La Serena, Chile or Rosario, Argentina (Participatory District Council). These Councils do not have representatives from specific sectors such as housing, health or education, etc.

FILE 17 · THE DEMOCRATISATION OF LOCAL GOVERNANCE

---

1 From core document (insert exact reference)

(ii) Increasing responsibilities and powers for existing organisations

There is a second mechanism that was identified while analysing PB at the beginning of the 2000s in some cities such as Montevideo, Uruguay or Cuenca but which is not particularly visible in any of the 12 examples. It relates to broadening the mandate of social organisations (for example, the Montevideo *Neighbours' Councils,* called *Consejos Vecinales)* or for political organisations like the Parish Councils in Cuenca) which in addition to their usual activities will, from now on, become involved in participatory budgeting. They will integrate the participatory budgeting process into their activities and their decision-making functions.

(iii) Non-institutionalised dynamic processes

In some of the more recent initiatives and mainly in European and American cities, such as Cascais, Portugal or Chicago, there are no institutionalised or formalised Councils or Community based bodies. Therefore, *"leadership committees"* created in Chicago's District 49 remain informal and can be joined by volunteers committed to the PB process and who wish to become more involved. In this case, participatory budgeting tends to foster commitment from neighbourhood's residents, who, in time, might become committee members.

2. Multi-actor governance and the building of new entities among diverse stakeholders

In the previous section, attention was paid to entities which are essentially community organisations created during the participatory budgeting process and made up of elected citizens, both male and female. A second type of organisation comprising not only of citizens but made up jointly of civil society/public sector and, at times, involving other stakeholders, such as the private sector will also be addressed in this document. These organisations are much more common than ten years ago . They could highlight the influence of the concept of good governance, with its purpose to forge better relations for dialogue and decision-making among stakeholders interested in urban issues.

(i) Joint civil society/government entities

One approach is to create joint councils made up of representatives from civil societies and government (city councils and sometimes elected officials). The Local and Provincial Coordination Council in Ilo is a good example of this type of governance entity.

(ii) Specific multi-actor entities

A second approach is to have ad-hoc organisations comprising of a large number of various types of stakeholders. These organisations, described below, are increasing in number and are becoming more complex:

- **The Participatory Budgeting Monitoring Committee for Secondary Schools** in the Nord-Pas-de-Calais Region (see File 14) is not only limited to secondary school students alone although the majority of the committee members are students. At least half of the members must be students, i.e. eight of the 15 members. The remaining seven are either members of the teaching, administrative, technical or health staff, parents or any other person affiliated with the school or belong to what Regional Authorities refer to as the "educational community". In other words, all stakeholders must be involved in the educational field. This is a significant innovation in the area of democratic governance.

- **The Municipal Advisory Forum**, currently in place in Dondo, Mozambique, has been evolving, transforming and becoming stronger in the last 15 years (see file on Dondo for more details). This attests to the complex nature of the Forum and the ingenuity of the local people to build a multi-actor model from the rubble of a deadly and protracted civil war. The binding force and raison d'être of this model was and continues to be participatory budgeting. It should be recalled here that the Advisory Forum, made up of 75 members, brings together community leaders, religious leaders, representatives of grassroots organisations such as organisations for women and young people, influential people at the local level and economic agents.

- **The Participatory Budgeting Council** of Yaoundé 6 brings together, under the chairmanship of the Mayor, representatives of the Executive branch of the commune, civil society and representatives from the economic sector. The participation of the latter is not commonplace and is related to the community being willing to make participatory budgeting the driving force behind wealth creation and economic development.

(iii) Community Pillar AND multi-actor governance structure

What appears noteworthy in experiences seen in Dondo, Ilo and even Belo Horizonte – and these are not the only ones – is that participatory budgeting has enabled community and citizens' entities to be created and strengthened along with a sense of greater autonomy. In addition, it allowed for governance entities in which representatives from these newly created community based entities can play a greater role.

- In Dondo, the joint **Municipal Advisory Forum** must include Development committees from each district, led by the civic educators; development committees in 51 districts and community councils

- Similarly the **Provincial Coordination Council** and the **Permanent Participatory Budgeting Commission** in Ilo only make sense as areas for dialogue and democratic governance entities if they are deemed community spaces created for and by participatory budgeting: **The Participatory Budgeting Board** [*Mesa Directiva del Presupuesto Participativo*] made up of six elected members from the 400 participating organisations; the **PB Oversight Committee**; the **Project Management Committees** for projects decided on in the participatory budgeting framework and the neighbour assemblies [*juntas vecinales*].

- The **Municipal Housing Council** in Belo Horizonte, Brazil that is key in the implementation of the Participatory Budgeting for Housing process is made up of (see document on Belo Horizonte) 20 representatives from various backgrounds such as trade unions, businesses, legislative and executive branches of government and five representatives from the people's housing movement. Here again a new multi-actor governance entity emerged. However, in addition, like in previous examples, several wholly autonomous citizen-led entities that have been established, the Comforças in particular, are comprised of representatives elected during the the Regional PB Forums. The Ethics Committee is part of the Municipal Housing Forum and composed of Comforças members. Its main role is to investigate complaints of any irregularities throughout the process.

Cities with Participatory budgeting processes aiming to radically democratise democracy and to build "another possible city " are those that at the same time, *on one hand* and first and foremost, strengthen citizen/community power and its autonomy and, *on the other,* create bodies [or entities] such as forums or round tables [*mesas de concertación*] where various stakeholders such as government, businesses, universities or trade unions can engage in dialogue. It should be noted that even though the Forums are open to citizens, if there is no capacity building occurring simultaneously of the citizens' movement; if its ability to express itself and to make its voice heard is not being strengthened, the weaker the forums will become over time. The risk of citizens' representatives being co-opted is high and they often serve to "show that democracy is at work" and that civil society is present. This situation occurs often in participatory budgeting where the aim is merely to improve governance (see file 2 on underlying logics at work in PB).

3. Lessons and advantages

These two types of organisations, community organisations such as "Participatory Budgeting Councils" and Multi-Actor entities such as the "Multi-Stakeholders Forum" and "City wide Councils" do not contradict each other but are, instead, complementary. As mentioned in the document on continuity in the PB process, they seek to be better **rooted** in the fertile breeding ground of civil society in the broadest sense, and to be better **anchored** into the city's administrative structure, the municipal council, formal and informal businesses and people's movements and organisations.

There are two distinct advantages of these forms of greater democratic governance seen and experienced in participatory budgeting processes:

- The first is building or rebuilding trust and dialogue among citizens themselves, on one hand, but also, and in particular, between elected officials and civil servants and people who no longer trust politicians – and in the vast majority of cases with just cause- or politics, which is serious from the perspective of bringing about positive change in society (see file on Cascais that addresses this issue).

- The second is improving the social environment among stakeholders involved, clearly illustrated in the file on participatory budgeting in secondary schools in the Nord-Pas-de-Calais region in France that highlights this change as a significant benefit that is difficult to quantify. The school environment has changed and relationships among students and adults have become calmer; secondary school students, parents, members of the technical, administrative and teaching staff understand each other better and there are, therefore, fewer acts of aggression and vandalism than before.

4. Limitations and open question

The organisations and institutions mentioned appear very complex in nature and are time and energy consuming for deciding, at the end of the day on limited public resources in spite of existing wealth. If these entities do not allow for progress to be made to ensure greater control over a larger percentage of public, private, local, national and international resources, then they are fighting a losing battle. The challenge, then, is to scale up and move towards prioritising and controlling resources. At this level, these institutions can indeed promise a future in which other cities are possible.

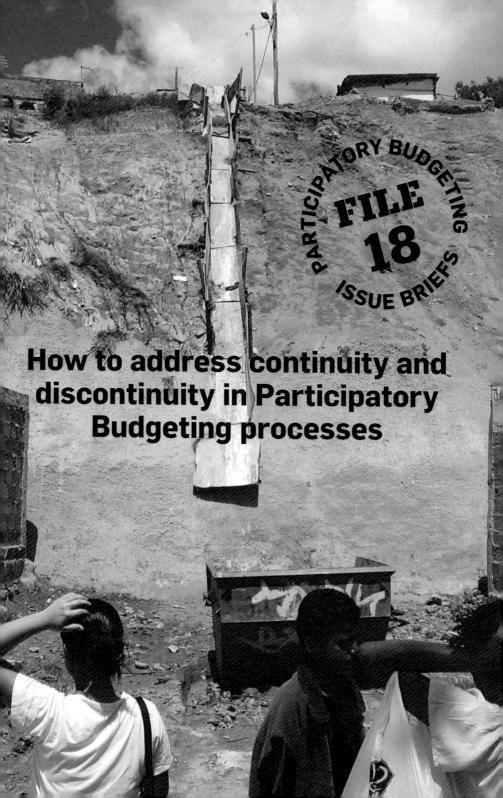

PARTICIPATORY BUDGETING

FILE

18

ISSUE BRIEFS

How to address continuity and discontinuity in Participatory Budgeting processes

How to address continuity and discontinuity in Participatory Budgeting processes

Author
Cabannes, Yves
ycabanes@mac.com

Date
2/2014 [French]
8/2014 [English]
Update 4/2017

Despite the increasing number of cities making use of Participatory Budgeting – approximately 2500 in 2017 – many face the challenge of ensuring **continuity and sustainability in the long term.** There is no collective memory for PB processes that developed in different directions, were interrupted, or definitively come to an end. Three situations can be identified and each raises various questions which to date remain, for the most part, unanswered:

Situation 1: Disruption of the Participatory Budgeting process during a political mandate

An evaluation of the situation in Brazil shows that during the legislative term 1997-2000, more than 20% of the 103 PB experiences that had begun in 1997 had not continued and had come to a halt before the end of the municipal mandate. The "volatility" of some PB processes is not only seen in Brazil. This also occurred during the first PB experience in Maputo, Mozambique. Disruptions to the process raise several questions: Why was the process disrupted? What did not work well? What adverse effects did this have at the local level? Was the process ever resumed?

Situation 2: Continuity in the Participatory Budgeting process in spite of a radical change of political parties in power

This occurred, for example, in Porto Alegre where the Workers' Party lost elections after 16 years in power, and in Caixas do Sul in the same state of Rio Grande do Sul, the birthplace of participatory budgeting.

After a period of fierce opposition or reticence, participatory budgeting continued as the hallmark of both cities and spurred political rhetoric of the new governments in power. In other Latin American cities, such as in Ilo, Peru and in Cuenca, Ecuador, the participatory budgeting process is on-going, indeed has been strengthened, despite changes in political parties in power[1]. Continuity of PB processes in a changing political climate raises the issue of whether or not explanations citing the people's lobby as the reason for participatory budgeting's continuation are sufficient to fully understand why the PB process still functions. It also raises questions about the nature of ongoing processes, above and beyond still being referred to as "participatory budgeting". It is for this reason that the tools for analysis suggested in File 2 are critical for understanding any possible changes in direction and their underpinning logic.

Situation 3: Disruptions in PB experiences amid political change

This is an occurrence that is, unfortunately, more widespread than the previous situations just described. It occurred in many Brazilian cities such as Sao Paulo[2], Belem and in smaller ones like Icapui and Barra Mansa[3]. This also occurred in Africa and in Seville, as described in this book. More often than not, participatory budgeting does not withstand changes in political power. These examples raise some further questions: Are there preconditions to ensure minimal continuity? What are the minimum precautions to be taken? What should be done to ensure that this process is irreversible above and beyond the political will of one Mayor or another or the activism of a citizen's movement, which is quite often transitory?

To address these issues, it is important to clarify what it means to have a process that is sustainable in the long term: Should there be an independent **PB process** or a **participation policy that includes** PB? Or should a completely different type of **political** democracy **project** be launched in which participatory budgeting is merely the initial stage or a component within a larger framework?

FILE 18 · CONTINUITY AND DISCONTINUITY

---

1 Extract from an article that appeared in two magazines: "Mouvements" and "Territoire" entitled "Les budgets participatifs en Amérique Latine. De Porto Alegre à l'Amérique Centrale, en passant par la zone andine: tendances, défis et limites, Cabannes, Y. 2006)
2 Symbolic due to its size and the original approach used
3 Where original Participatory Budgeting experiences with children and young people were strengthened

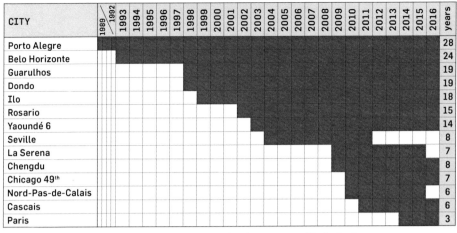

Timeframe of Participatory Budgeting in the cities and regions presented in the book.
Source: local teams; Processing of data: Cabannes / Delgado, 2017

Lessons drawn from PB experiences

The central argument in this document is divided into two key issues: institutional **anchoring** on one hand, and a process becoming as **deeply grounded as possible** within citizens' movements on the other. Before exploring this further, here is a recap of the PB experiences mentioned in this book.

The graph above shows the PB process in the long term for the 13 experiences mentioned, above and beyond Porto Alegre, a milestone and the most enduring PB process. This sample does not reflect the variety of PB processes underway or that have occurred in the past, and long-lasting experiences are over-represented here. However, there are several experiences that have been consolidated through time and that have withstood political power changing hands as occurred in Porto Alegre, Belo Horizonte or Ilo, Peru and more recently in Yaoundé 6th Commune. Nonetheless, despite institutional integration of the PB process and its apparent robustness, the process in Seville did not weather changes in power from left to right and the PB process has been disrupted.

To make progress in the debate on continuity and to ensure that PB experiences are sustainable in the long term, three processes, spanning three continents - Ilo, Peru; Chengdu, China and Participatory Budgeting with secondary school students in the Nord-Pas-de-Calais Region in France - appear to be particularly good examples.

Ilo, the consolidation of participatory budgeting in a close-knit society

In spite of changes of political parties in power, Ilo PB has managed to sustain itself since 1999 and is the longest running experience in Peru. It is celebrating 19 years in 2017. For Mario Villavicencio Ramirez, currently at the City Strategic Planning Directorate and directly involved in PB process since its inception, there are two main reasons to explain why PB experiences are ongoing despite the many obstacles described in the file on Ilo:

"Empowerment of people has been and remains the primary factor in achieving sustainable participatory budgeting in Ilo: when the process was launched in 1999, a civil society forum was put into place called the Participatory Budgeting Board [Mesa Directiva], made up of civil society representatives. It assumed and continues to assume the role of honouring agreements in each of the processes. In 2003, there was an attempt to disown the process and to dissolve the Participatory Budgeting Board, but the voices of the leaders were heard and in the end the participatory budgeting process was allowed to continue.
Participatory Budgeting began, four years before a National Law was passed. In August 2003, the Participatory Budget Framework Law 28056 was drafted. This law was spearheaded by Member of Parliament, Ernesto Herrera Becerra, former Mayor of Ilo."[4]

According to Mr. Villavicencio, the national law on participatory budgeting, often harshly criticised because its provisions are deemed too rigid, has been a factor that enhanced stability and the rooting of participatory budgeting within institutions. It was passed at a time when the local PB process was under threat.

Is it likely that the Chengdu PB experience, quite innovative within the Chinese context, could be disrupted?

In the course of several trips, research and interviews with local decision-makers, carried out between 2008 and 2013, one of the recurring questions addressed whether or not Chengdu's experience with PB and its 40,000 projects decided upon by villagers, ran the risk of coming to an end, given that it seemed "too good to be true..." From observations, it appears that:

---

4 Interviews and discussions with the authors, December 2013 and January 2014

"PB in Chengdu is not at risk, at least not for the foreseeable future. Similar mechanisms to village councils have been experimented with in many other parts of China as one of many grassroots democracy innovations. Moreover, Chengdu is a pilot zone for exploring solutions for balanced development. In addition, social and land conflicts have been reduced here in a peaceful way, so the central government may want to see more of these experiments. The significant increase in the resources allocated to PB each year and the expansion of the approach into urban communities are good indications of the consolidation of the process. In addition, those who wanted to cut the loans linked to PB encountered serious obstacles, and this part of the programme has been strengthened.

Policy makers and Party bureaucrats were very strategic in making these PB practices in Chengdu difficult to reverse. Revoking them would involve covering the repayment of the loans that villagers had contracted. This is a complicated decision for any politician, as his or her mandate is for a maximum of five years, and he or she could not commit that easily to resources beyond this term, much less deal with the social and political turmoil that such a decision would entail."[5]

Two main factors seem to explain the limited risk of discontinuity: on one hand sound integration within a significant public policy and within the administrative structure, and on the other hand, ensuring that the PB process is deeply rooted in villages struggling for a greater level of democracy and better living conditions. In 2017, PB in Chengdu remains alive and well, and expanded over recent years from villages to urban districts. Hard facts clearly demonstrates that "PB in Chengdu is not at risk" became a reality.

Participatory budgeting in secondary schools: internalisation of the process within various administrative structures, and broadening political scope

Could the relatively recent and increasingly popular participatory budgeting experience in secondary schools in the Nord-Pas-de-Calais Region be sustained if another political party came to office? The Vice President of the Regional Authorities for Participatory Democracy, who initiated the process, addresses this risk:

5 Cabannes and Ming, *Participatory budgeting at scale and bridging the rural-urban divide in Chengdu*, Environment & Urbanization, 2013, International Institute for Environment and Development (IIED). Vol 26(1): 257–275

"The process must be owned by all stakeholders and institutions concerned and not be imposed. Anchoring is important for us. We are committed to having regional services in the driving seat and spearheading the process. The first year requires our support to work on the methodology, produce the first set of tools and put some monitoring device in place. During the second year the Directorate of Finance and Investment (DFI) takes the lead through a Project Director, and in the third year a fully fledge team mainstreams the process in other regional services, primarily Heritage".

At the political level, there is a similar will to look for broader political support and appropriation: "The PB process in secondary schools is not only led by Myriam Cau, who was elected head of Participative Democracy, Sustainable Development and Evaluation." It is also led by The Vice President of Secondary Schools in the Steering Committee composed of secondary school authorities, the National Federation representing of parents of students, CESER (Regional Economic, Social and Environmental Council), DRAAF (Regional Directorate for Food, Agriculture and Forests), representatives of Principals and secondary school students[6]. Regional elected representatives of the Board of Directors of Secondary Schools are also involved[7]. In addition, participatory budgeting in secondary schools is requested by the institutions themselves. They too are volunteers, not for any additional financial resources that PB might bring (PB resources for secondary schools come from the Multiannual Investment Programme) but because it creates a dynamic that mobilises the entire educational community, and in particular, secondary school students. As occurred in Chengdu, for example, commitment above and beyond politics is considered important: "the PB process in the secondary schools spans a period of 2 years, so that even if any political changes occur, such as the ones caused by elections during this period, the process launched prior to this will continue to have an impact."
One might wonder if it is desirable for PB to continue in spite of changes in parties in power. There again, responses to this question differs significantly among those preferring to get rid of the model to ensure that it is not co-opted or perverted and those who support it, and these are the majority. They believe that PB should continue, regardless of the political

---

6 Interviews and correspondence between Myriam Cau, Marie Helene and Yves Cabannes, Jan 2014
7 Ibid.

party in power and be a forum for resistance and countervailing power given its benefits. Those in charge of the Nord-Pas-de-Calais region are very clear on the issue:

"YES! This is what we want because experience has shown that this process engages young secondary school students in the Steering Committee, who clearly express that that are indeed interested. They appreciate that they are allowed to voice their opinions and that the projects they vote on are implemented. This shows them that commitments can be honoured by elected officials."[8]

8 Interviews and correspondence between Myriam Cau, Marie Helene and Yves Cabannes, Jan 2014

Recommendations to further radicalise PB - Part one

Citizen and public sector participation

PARTICIPATORY BUDGETING

FILE

19

ISSUE BRIEFS

Recommendations to further radicalise PB - Part one: Citizen and public sector participation

Author
Cabannes, Yves
ycabanes@mac.com

Date
February 2014 [French]
August 2014 [English]

One of the keys to understanding the PB experiences presented in file 2 is that they respond to very diverse underlying rationales that vary from one city to another, and among stakeholders within the same city. Three main rationales were identified: (i) improving the efficiency of the public service and optimising the budgetary resources. The primary logic at work is technocratic management; (ii) improving the relationship between government and citizens and among other economic and social actors. In this case, the underlying rationale is primarily "good governance"; and finally (iii) radically democratising democracy, from a politically revolutionary perspective, through which citizen enact profound societal change through various mechanisms including participatory decision making.

As far as we are concerned, the political objective of radical democratisation remains probably the only rationale that genuinely contributes to building "other possible cities" and to generating alternatives to cities as commodities. The two first rationales are palliatives for the neoliberal system, serving simply to mitigate some of its injustices, and extending its lifespan. Information from some of the cities presented in this book clearly shows that radical PB processes are those that have generated closer links with the other alternatives identified in this series to the city as a commodity, whether it is by promoting employment or housing cooperative societies or

other methods of collective or community land ownership that allow inhabitants to remain on the land they live on, or by enhancing urban agriculture. The following examples illustrate some links between some radically democratic cases of PB and other alternatives from this series:

- The initial participatory budgeting phase in Belo Horizonte when the *Participatory Budgeting for Housing* process was set up as a result of pressure from self-managed (*autogestão*) homeless groups;
- The PB experience in Seville, spearheaded by "catalyst groups" (*grupos motores*) from social organisations and local activists;
- Rosario set up a participatory budgeting process just after the collapse of the neoliberal regime as a result of action by "*piqueteros*" (picketers);
- Some villages around Chengdu where residents appoint Village Councillors that do not belong to existing political structures and that have the capacity to make decision on the budget.

The main concluding recommendation of this book is to have an horizon composed of the "maximum arrangements" or most advanced arrangements for each of the 18 variables relating to participation, financial, legal, institutional or territorial participatory budgeting dimensions (see tables 1 and 2 in file 3). Therefore, this horizon can be painted through these 18 strokes. Even if none of the PB experiences feature all of the most advanced arrangements at any given time, some of these arrangements are visible at certain times in each example. This proves that they are not a figment of one's imagination but are indeed a reality. Having them all present in the same place at the same time is more difficult. This horizon line, will be drawn and described here, in relation to its participatory dimensions from both the citizens and the public sector. File 19 will address the other dimensions.

Citizen's participatory dimension

Variable 1. Forms of participation. With regard to the forms of participation: direct democracy and universal participation for all those "using" the city and not only people who live or sleep there. PB participation is opened in this maximum arrangement to all those who reside legally or illegally and to immigrants with or without official residence status. One part of the population is sometimes excluded, as is the case in Chengdu,

China, where only long-term residents – native *hukou* – are allowed to vote on PB priorities. Those who recently migrated to the city, even if they hold a residence certificate, and undocumented immigrants, cannot take part in the participatory budgeting decision-making process (see file 15 on Chengdu, the capital of Sichuan province).

Variable 2. The last body to approve the budget being deliberated: Citizens' assemblies make the decisions. These decisions are sovereign and "binding". The local legislative and executive branches of government or their equivalents ratify them. The people make these decisions after lengthy and genuinely open and democratic public deliberations on the projects proposed by citizens. It does not involve mere voting alone, but it restores a voice to citizens and enables them to deliberate, or to build dissensus instead of consensus around issues on which agreement has not been reached, as occurred in Seville.

Variable 3. Final body to determine budgetary priorities. Commissions composed of delegates elected during the PB assemblies make up the final budget matrix; they have authority and power over participatory budgeting decisions. The number of delegates is in proportion to the number of members in the assembly, such as in several cities in Brazil, and can be, in some cases, in excess of a thousand. These delegates elect the councillors: the more delegates there are, the more councillors there will be so that the diversity of citizens is better reflected. This approach is fundamentally different to the approach used in the system of representative democracy in which the number of city councillors is not related to the number of citizens *participating*.

Variable 4. Community participation or citizen participation. Participatory budgeting should prioritise and decide on projects or programmes for each level of space, that contribute towards citizens' identity: from their immediate neighbourhoods, to the districts and the city as a whole. This is the level of space that the majority of participatory budgeting experiences related to in this book. Nonetheless, PB should also earmark resources for intermediate levels such as districts. As is the case, for example, in Guarulhos or Belo Horizonte with "digital" budgets and to the city as a whole, as in Seville. The shift from participatory budgeting limited to local areas and *community* participation toward *citizen* participation, i.e. for large-scale investments at city level or in metropolitan areas, is key to turn the ideals of "another city is possible" into a reality.

Variable 5. Level of participation of marginalised groups. Sound, affirmative and specific measures should be taken to ensure that those who have never participated, those who are powerless, can also decide about their future and the future of their neighbourhoods and cities. Efforts targeting Latin Americans in Chicago's Ward 49; for young people and secondary school students in La Serena and the Nord-Pas-de-Calais region; for women in Rosario and for immigrants in Seville are some of the PB experiences that show that "it is possible" to overcome exclusion and marginalisation and that it is indeed vastly better for all citizens, for local government, and for the overall development of cities. Giving "actor-based" participatory budgeting the emphasis it deserves is one of the current challenges to contribute to long term sustainability of PB processes.

Variable 6. Oversight of project implementation. Oversight by the people with regard to the implementation of projects and programmes decided on during the PB process should be the general rule so that people can capitalise on gains made and any risks of diverting resources or delays can be minimised. This oversight works best when it is conducted by specific committees made up of elected representatives, as is the case in Belo Horizonte with the Comforças and in Chengdu which has monitoring committees that are set up through elected village councils.

Public participation dimension

Variable 7. Level of transparency in information and decision-making. Decisions made in assemblies on the content of projects selected (total amount, aim, start and end of project, location, must be clearly announced via posters, information and communication campaigns, special publications and supplements in local newspapers and the websites of mayors' offices and civil society organisations. Nonetheless, information made available by government, mayors' offices, regions, communes or districts should be widely disseminated and accessible to encourage or foster citizen participation. Quality information should be conveyed about projects that have been completed. This is the only way that citizens will build trust in the process and see that the number of hours spent on meetings and assemblies is well worth it.

Variable 8. *Extent to which approved projects have been completed (within 2 years).* One of the difficulties encountered by several cities, and this was the case in Rosario, Argentina and Belo Horizonte, Brazil; Dondo, Mozambique and Yaoundé 6, Cameroon, is the difficulty in implementating of projects that have already been decided on and approved, whether it is due to a lack of resources, lack of budget planning or unforeseen circumstances beyond the city's control. Regardless of the reason cited, the recommendation is that within two years after projects have been voted on, at least 80% of them should be, implemented and operational. Failing this, it is understandable that those who participated in the process will be genuinely disappointed and angry; these sentiments will be palpable in the streets and at the ballot box. In addition, many people will lose confidence in the participatory budgeting process and in its ability to turn the ideals of "another city is possible" into reality, and ensure that the city is not just another commodity.

Variable 9. Role of the legislative branch of government. The legislative branch of government plays a pivotal role and it is important for city councillors to be directly involved and understand that the success of the PB process depends heavily on their commitment. Some cities, such as Cascais, Portugal, have allowed those elected to become more involved. Likewise, elected representatives in the Nord-Pas-de-Calais region in France have been the driving force in promoting participatory budgeting for secondary school students. Above and beyond the political dimension, from a more practical standpoint, commitment from the legislative branch of government is a guarantee that the "PB budget matrix" will be ratified beyond political divides. In addition, as explained in the case of Ilo Peru (see file 11), the national law on participatory budgeting passed by the Parliament in Peru stemmed from the PB process in these very city neighbourhoods. This law, according to decision-makers in Ilo, has had a positive effect on sustaining and consolidating the PB experience, during political changes that could have brought it to an end.

Building a Pedagogy for Democratic Governance

The political will of government and citizens' organisations committed to the democratic radicalisation of participatory budgeting should be accompanied by a measure that emerges from the most advanced PB experiences related in this book. As mentioned by Pedro Pontual[1], participatory budgeting should be recognised as a "school for citizenship". One of the challenges lies in developing a method for teaching democratic governance, to enable civil society actors, activists and local governments to effectively play their role". Various cities have successfully developed in this direction:

- In Guarulhos, Brazil (file 7) PB is conducted with training and capacity building support from the Paulo Freire Institute (Institut Paulo Freire).
- In Rosario (file 10) a team from the local government worked closely with a number of community-led organisations and citizens involved in PB to develop and published a dictionary/glossary of key participatory budgeting concepts in order to inform the wider public about PB key concepts used all along the process.
- In Yaoundé 6 in Cameroon (file 13) the ASSOAL NGO work to reach out to each individual, often working in remote neighbourhoods;
- In the village of La Serena Chile, [who developed] the highly influential Participatory School of Social Leadership.

Together these illustrate some of the possible pathways toward achieving this radical objective. PB experiences for young people and children, in primary schools, secondary schools and in neighbourhoods and which are increasing in number, are also an example of how the PB process is contributing to a new civic culture.

---

1 Pedro Pontual worked with Paulo Freire in São Paulo and then as Coordinator of the school for citizenship at the Institut Polis. He was Chair for several years of the Education Council for Latin American Adults, CEEAL. He I was responsible for participatory budgeting in several cities in Brazil including Santo André. See article entitled "El presupuesto participative como escuela de ciudanía" la Era Urbana, 2004, pp 60-61

Recommendations to further radicalise PB - Part two

Links with other alternatives

PARTICIPATORY BUDGETING

FILE

20

ISSUE BRIEFS

Recommendations to further radicalise PB – Part two: Links with other alternatives

Author
Cabannes, Yves
ycabanes@mac.com

Date
February 2014 [French]
August 2014 [English]

Following on from file 18, this file presents the most advanced participatory budgeting arrangements that would enable the full transformative potential of the PB process to be achieved, allowing it to contribute fully to building alternatives to the city as a commodity. The document includes variables describing the different aspects of participatory budgeting: (i) financial, budgetary and fiscal; (ii) normative and institutional and (iii) physical or territorial. These dimensions and the variables are detailed in file 10 and illustrated with the experience of Rosario.

Financial, budgetary and fiscal dimensions

Variable 10. Amount of resources being debated. This should account for 100% of the investment budget, which is the case in a small number of cities such as Ilo (see file 11). Participatory budgeting should also address the entire operations budget for cities, districts or at the territorial level at which it is being implemented.

Variable 11. Municipal budget for participatory budgeting operations. A budget line should be determined to permanently cover four aspects over the long term: (i) financing of salaries of the team responsible and of department in charge of conducting PB;; (ii) a training and education budget for the people (see file 7 on Guarulhos), for city staff as well as representatives, councillors and participants

directly involved in the process; (iii) a communications budget to mobilise citizens and to keep them informed. This budget covers the publication of rules and regulations; information on projects selected in hard copy and online; and finally (iv), as in the case of the city of Seville (file12), a budget for outsourcing studies, research and evaluations to be conducted to universities and NGOs. The cost/benefit ratio of such budget allocations is generally very positive.

Variable 12. Deliberations on taxation policies and practices. The definition and the prioritisation of taxation policies ensure, at the end of the day, the level of resources available within local and regional authorities. This definition should be one of the prerogatives of participatory budgeting. In addition, all of the loans to be contracted by local and regional authorities should be discussed during the PB process. That was one of the innovations introduced by Porto Alegre and one that is often forgotten. It is extremely important because the repayment of national and international loans, either public or private, is generally deducted from the resources allocated to participatory budgeting.

Normative and institutional dimensions

Variable 13. Degree of institutionalisation. One of the challenges of participatory budgeting lies in finding a balance between two elements that are a constant source of tension. Firstly, a legal or juridical framework/structure that guarantees the sustainability of PB even when new governments in power are opposed to the process and which also guarantees participation as a right. Secondly, strict legalisation established by decree or by laws of all the rules and regulations would not be beneficial because it would stifle the dynamic processes at work. From the perspective of "radical democratisation of democracy", the ability of citizens to determine the rules of the game; the cycle; meeting times and venues; the criteria for allocation of available resources and the membership of the Participatory Budgeting Council appears critical. Too much legislation inhibits the dynamics of participation and the emergence and flow of new ideas. Insufficient legislation, on the other hand, could, at certain times, weaken these dynamics. (See file 17 on the continuity and discontinuity of PB processes in several cities presented). The yearly definition and updating of internal rules of procedure, by PB delegates and councillors, known as "*auto-reglamentados*" (self determined rules) in Seville, or "*regimento interno*" (rules of procedure) in Guarulhos and Belo Horizonte is a good example of the space for freedom that should be left to citizens.

Variable 14. Instrumental or Participatory rationale. To release its transformative potential, participatory budgeting must be part of a wider a democratic system, in which participation is considered a right, exercised in several spaces and approaches. Without a wider culture of participative democracy, the socio-political impact of PB is limited. Participatory budgeting is one amongst a range of modalities that can play a central role in a system of participation; others include referendums, termination of mandate, neighbourhood councils, participatory planning, right of initiative, round tables, etc. It is important, at the local level, to define the expected value added by a PB process and determine its place in a system and renewed culture of participation.

Variable 15. Relations with planning instruments. To fully play its role, as a planning mechanism, participatory budgeting must develop clear relationships and specific types of interaction with other planning instruments that are city specific: spatial planning, sectoral planning, and strategic planning amongst others, in the short-term and long-term. In other words, participatory budgeting, as an advanced arrangement, must be at the same time in line with the system of participation (see previous item) and be an integral part of the planning system. This type of integration depends, *inter alia*, on how broader participation bodies and norms are defined, known in some cities as City Councils, in which the body created for participatory budgeting is only one component. The Advisory Forum in Dondo (see file 8) is another example in which participatory budgeting and planning are both part of the same dynamic.

Physical (or territorial dimension)

This dimension is particularly noticeable significant when considering the potential of participatory budgeting for building alternative cities, by and for citizens, and where physical/territorial justice would go hand in hand with social justice.

Variable 16. Degree of "infra-municipal" decentralisation. In an advanced arrangement, participatory budgeting deepens public debate above and beyond the existing administrative structures. It grants citizens from all districts, including the most marginalised, the authority to make decisions on how to use public money to improve their situation in the short and long-term. Yaoundé 6 (see file 13) is an good example of the "spatial" deepening of democracy towards all disadvantaged neighbourhoods in the Commune. It should be noted that this does not mean, however, that resources will only be allocated to improving the neighbourhood itself. It is recommended that a percentage of the resources be used for projects at city level. These projects are to be determined by residents in neighbourhoods, however remote they are. This is the direction given to decentralisation as a political process that reverses priorities.

Variable 17. Degree of inclusion of the city's rural areas. The resources deliberated should not be limited to urbanised zones alone but should include all urban, peri-urban and rural areas. Affirmative action prioritising rural areas above the number of inhabitants, which is often low, is critical to reversing physical priorities. Chengdu's metropolitan area in China is an excellent example that demonstrates how participatory budgeting that began in rural and peri-urban areas has begun to address the rural divide that had widened over the last thirty years.

Variable 18. Degree of inversion of territorial priorities. Resources for participatory budgeting should be prioritised for areas in the city where needs are most pressing and not only for neighbourhoods where investments would be the most productive from an economic and commodity-based perspective. Allocating and channeling a high percentage of PB resources to areas where needs are greatest has been particularly successful in the city of Belo Horizonte (see file 6) which became a reference for other cities. The Urban Quality of Life Index (IQVU) allows measuring quality of life in all neighbourhoods and districts of the city. The lower the quality of life of a given area the higher the level of resources that it will receive. It is to be noted that the amounts received are still small in comparison to the city budget or in comparison to the scale of the inhabitants' needs. (See file 3 that compares the resources deliberated per inhabitant per year in several cities)

Only three variables were presented here to work on the physical dimension but others are possible and relevant. This is the case, for example, for a variable that relates PB aimed at improving public spaces. These spaces are privatised and marketed and are their improvement is excellent example of the contribution that participatory budgeting makes to the concept of the city not being a commodity. Because of participatory budgeting, the majority of cities mentioned in this book have improved public spaces, at neighbourhoods or districts levels as desired by inhabitants.

Final recommendation on the links between PB and other alternatives

The main recommendation to conclude this book on participatory budgeting is that local and regional authorities that implement PBs and social organisations and civil society activists that struggle to improve them, should lobby to have PB funding available for urban agriculture projects and programmes; housing and employment cooperative societies; social economy projects; and collective or community land ownership and use, such as *"community land trusts"*.

In addition, budgetary resources allocated to programmes voted as priorities by PB assemblies should not be spent only in the country's national currency. These resources instead can serve as a reserve currency to enable local and complementary currencies to be issued. These locally emitted local currencies could in turn foster the emergence of community banks using local currencies. Local businesses in charge of project implementation could as well be paid for their services with this newly created local currency.

Participatory budgeting has an enormous potential to bridge up with the other avenues leading to "other possible cities": urban agriculture; local currencies; community land trusts and collective and community-based land ownership; housing and employment cooperative societies and alternatives to eviction. Some of them are under construction and were presented in this book. Many more will come.

Part 4

RESOURCE FILES

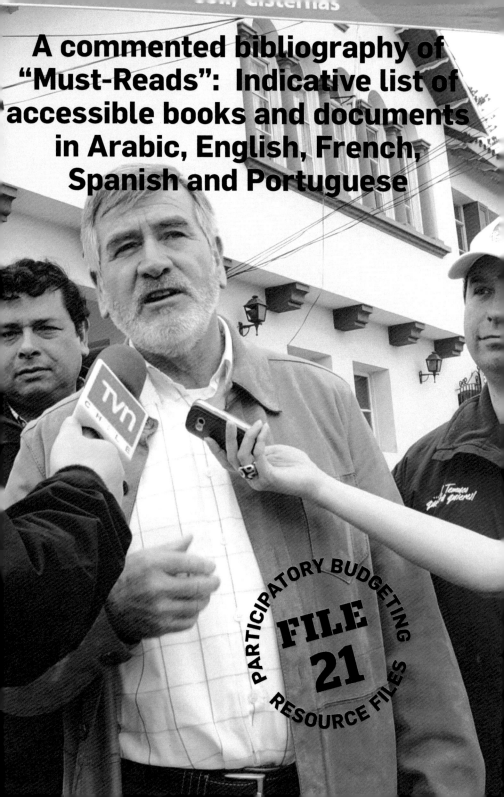

A commented bibliography of "Must-Reads": Indicative list of accessible books and documents in Arabic, English, French, Spanish and Portuguese

PARTICIPATORY BUDGETING
FILE
21
RESOURCE FILES

Commented bibliography of "Must-Reads": Indicative list of accessible books and documents in Arabic, English, French, Spanish and Portuguese

Authors
Cabannes, Yves
ycabanes@mac.com
Delgado, Cecília
cmndelgado@gmail.com

Date
03/2014
Update 4/2017

This file is organized in four sections: the first introduces general and critical texts; the second focuses on experiences; the third section proposes some evaluations; and the last section indicates some useful manuals, legal tools and methods. This is a limited selection to which many more valuable texts could have been added.

Language availability
Arabic: xxi, xxii
English: i, iii, iv, vii, xi, xvi, xviii, xxi, xxiii
French: i, iii, v, xi, xxi, xxii, xxiii, xxiv
Spanish: iii, v, vi, vii, ix, x, xiii, xvii, xix, xxi, xxv
Portuguese: ii, iii, v, viii, xii, xiv, xvi, xviii, xx, xxi, xxiii, xvi

A – General and introductory texts

(i) Allegretti, G, Herzberg, C, Sintomer, Y, with the collaboration of Röcke, A and Alves, M, **Participatory budgeting worldwide – updated version, study Nº 25,** Dialog Global, published by Engagement Global gGmbH - Service für Entwicklungsinitiativen (Global Civic Engagement - Service for Development Initiatives) Service Agency Communities in One World, Bonn, 2013, 96 pp

This essay on the dissemination and diversity of PB is designed to facilitate intercultural exchange between committed citizens, civil servants, experts and researchers. It identifies and explains different procedures, describes how and why they arose and illustrates the analysis with concrete examples. Specific tools such as transparent budgets, allocation criteria and/or websites are presented, and potential objectives of PB are clarified. This is not to say that any rigid blueprints will be provided. The essay is rather designed for use as a toolbox. We will not paint a more favorable picture of PB than the reality warrants. Both difficulties and success stories will be presented for what they are. It is only by clearly identifying challenges that the likelihood of responding to them successfully will increase [extract from authors' study presentation]. Available in French and in English.

http://portugalparticipa.pt/upload_folder/table_data/c3164679-c343-4715-b198-576aee3d4ad1/files/dialog-global.pdf

(ii) Avritzer, L.; Navarro Z. (orgs.). **A inovação democrática no Brasil: o orçamento participativo,** Cortez Editora, São Paulo, 2003, 334 pp

El libro contiene los resultados de una investigación sobre las diversas experiencias de presupuesto participativo existentes en Brasil, a partir de cuatro variables: tradición asociativa pre-existente, formato institucional, voluntad política y capacidad financiera del municipio. Se llega a un cuadro diversificado de 103 experiencias, algunas urbanas y otras rurales, la mayoría en ciudades pequeñas, concentradas especialmente en las regiones del Sur y Sureste brasileños. El lector comprende qué es el presupuesto participativo, cuáles son sus posibilidades de éxito, y por qué es importante su vinculación con una buena base asociativa. (Extractos de la contraportada del libro).

http://www.cortezeditora.com.br/DetalheProduto.aspx?ProdutoId=84f86a9e-d7b3-e011-955f-842b2b1656e4

(iii) Cabannes, Y; Baierle, S. **Municipal Government of Porto Alegre. Municipal Finance and Participatory Budgeting.** Base Document. Launching Seminar of URB-AL NETWORK No. 9, 2005, 104 pp

Launched at the start of the 2000s, whilst approximately 250 PB processes were underway, this is one of the first systematic analysis of PB, comparing 25 Latin American and European experiences. Informed by research and protagonists' opinions, this document illustrates a considerable number of issues that were discussed within the URBAL PB and municipal finance network, coordinated by Porto Alegre, which between 2000 and 2006 involved around 400 cities and organisations. The experience of Porto Alegre is introduced in the second chapter. Available in English, French, Portuguese and Spanish. A second comparison referring to 30 cities was carried out a couple of years later and published in Portuguese only.

http://www.centrourbal.com/sicat2/documentos/70_2007312920_R9-db-eng.pdf

(iv) Dias, Nelson (Organization), **Hope for Democracy. 25 Years of Participatory Budgeting Worldwide.** In Loco Association (Edition). April 2014, 495 pp

"This book represents the effort of more than forty authors and many other direct and indirect contributors that spread across different continents seek to provide an overview on the Participatory Budget (PB) in the World. They do so from very different backgrounds. Some are researchers, others are consultants, and others are activists connected to several groups and social movements. The texts reflect this diversity of approaches and perspectives well, and we do not try to influence that.
Therefore, this book is not the result of a comparative PB study from different parts of the world, though some authors have based their articles on the research in which they are involved. What we propose is an open and constructive reflection on the multiple dynamics of Participatory Budgets, challenging our readers to continue this work in their own realities." Source: Democratic Hope. Introduction by Nelson Dias (pag 13)

http://www.in-loco.pt/upload_folder/edicoes/1279dd27-d1b1-40c9-ac77-c75f31f82ba2.pdf

(v) Genro, Tarso; De Souza, Ubiratan. **Presupuesto Participativo: la experiencia de Porto Alegre.** CTA; EUDEBA, Buenos Aires, 1998, 123 pp

This is only available in French and Spanish, however it

is included in the English review, as it is one of the first books on the experience of the participatory budgeting in Porto Alegre, written by two of the most influential players. This experience was a significant turning point for participatory budgeting, from the author's standpoint, as for the first time, local government was not alone in allocating public funds. This turning point saw the creation of a new decision making model, by which the Executive and Legislative branches of local government, along with ordinary citizens, made decisions in a "new public space". As a result PB democratised political action and encouraged citizens to be more demanding and critical on the exercise of citizenship. Available in French: **Quand les habitants gèrent vraiment leur ville. Le Budget Participatif: l'expérience de Porto Alegre au Brésil.** Dossier Pour un Débat N°82, Editions Charles Léopold Mayer, Paris, 1998, 103p. Available in Spanish: **Presupuesto Participativo: la experiencia de Porto Alegre.** CTA; EUDEBA, Buenos Aires, 1998, 123p.

http://www.amazon.co.uk/El-Presupuesto-Participativo-experiencia-Alegre/dp/8476283199

(vi) Molina Molina, José. **Los Presupuestos Partici-pativos. Un modelo para priorizar objetivos y gestionar eficientemente en la Administración Local.** Editorial Aranzadi & Thomson Reuters, 2011, 425 pp

Ofrece un panorama inusitado, con informaciones sobre todo extraídas de Internet sobre procesos de democratización de los presupuestos participativos en el mundo. Se trata de un panorama único y de fácil acceso al lector, fruto de la recopilación y ordenación de una información dispersa, principalmente sobre los ámbitos administrativos y financieros de los presupuestos participativos, dos dimensiones sorprendentemente poco estudiadas con relación a la dimensión participativa ciudadana. El análisis realizado, desde esa perspectiva, permite vislumbrar las contribuciones existentes y potenciales de los PPs para modernizar las obsoletas maquinarias administrativas, las cuales están poco acostumbradas a procesos participativos y a un dialogo estrecho con la ciudadanía.

http://www.abebooks.co.uk/servlet/SearchResults?paratrk=&isbn=9788499030050&ltrec=t&bi=

(vii) **The Urban Era.** Global City Magazine. March 2004, Urban Management Programme **Special Edition on Participatory Budgeting,** Quito, 84 pp

"This book represents the effort of more than forty authors and many other direct and indirect contributors that spread across different continents seek to provide an overview on the Participatory Budget (PB) in the World. They do so from very different backgrounds. Some are researchers, others are consultants, and others are activists connected to several groups and social movements. The texts reflect this diversity of approaches and perspectives well, and we do not try to influence that. Therefore, this book is not the result of a comparative PB study from different parts of the world, though some authors have based their articles on the research in which they are involved. What we propose is an open and constructive reflection on the multiple dynamics of Participatory Budgets, challenging our readers to continue this work in their own realities." Source: "Spotlight on Knowledge. Evidence and lessons from Latin America". Area Governance. Theme Budget and Public policies, Fundar, Centro de Análisis e investigación, n/d. English version: CITEGO site / digital library / participatory budgeting

For Spanish http://www.rosario.gov.ar/sitio/verArchivo?id=4346&tipo=objetoMultimedia

(viii) Sánchez, Félix. **Orçamento Participativo teoria e prática.** Cortez Editora, São Paulo, 2002, 119 PP

El texto se orienta a debatir las innovaciones democráticas ocurridas a partir de la creación del Presupuesto Participativo (PP). Para ello, se hace un rescate y la crítica de las experiencias de participación democrática que culminaron en la creación del PP. Se discuten también la estructuración y los contornos organizacionales y políticos que presentan tales innovaciones. El documento esboza un escenario de relación entre el PP y la democracia participativa y deliberativa en la sociedad actual, e introduce una breve reflexión sobre la experiencia de la ciudad de São Paulo en el 2001.

http://www.cortezeditora.com.br/Index.aspx?Busca=Orcamento%2525Participativo%2525teoria%2525e%2525pratica&Tipo=0

B – Books related to experiences

(ix) Carillo Cano, A, Francés García, F, **Cuando la ciudadanía toma parte. La experiencia del presupuesto participativo de Petrer, España,** Preparación Ediciones – Proceso-Participación-Democracia, 2015, 97 pp. Creative Commons.

Esta monografía es hasta cierto atípica: fue co-escrita por los propios responsables del PP y relata la experiencia bastante innovadora del presupuesto participativo de Petrer, implementado entre los años 2003 y 2007. Trae interesantes reflexiones sobre la interrupción de proceso, lo cual es poco común, y toma el tiempo de hacer un balance detallado y critico a varios niveles: técnico, político, de gobierno y asociativo. Se apunta este trabajo porque la mayoría de los procesos de presupuestos participativos no se documentan, y todavía menos de forma crítica. Esto es particularmente el caso con aquellos que desaparecen y todavía más con los que se materializan en ciudades pequeñas o medianas, como Petrer, un municipio de la Provincia de Alicante que cuenta con unos 35.000 habitantes.

http://www.eparticipa.com/ES/seccion/descarga/repo/repofile_55e86219188e1

(x) Ford, Alberto. **El presupuesto participativo en Rosario: Una apuesta renovada al experimentalismo democrático, Intendencia de Rosario, Argentina,** Programa Urbal. 2009, 81 pp

El libro " El presupuesto participativo en Rosario, una apuesta renovada al experimentalismo democrático" nos parece de singular interés por lo menos tres razones: la primera por la precisión y la calidad de su contenido; la segunda por el proceso a través del cual fue escrito y producido y la tercera porque pone a la luz de manera brillante las facetas más innovadoras de unas de las experiencias de PP, que a pesar de sus limites, se singulariza por su calidad, su grado de consolidación y por sus alcances "[extracto del prologo a la primera edición, Cabannes, Y]

http://www.rosario.gov.ar/sitio/verArchivo?id=4322&tipo=objetoMultimedia

(xi) Gret, M and Sintomer, Y, **The Porto Alegre Experiment: Learning Lessons for Better Democracy,** London: Zed Books and Toronto: Fernwood 2005

"With its experiment in participative budget-making over the past decade, Porto Alegre has institutionalized the direct democratic involvement, locality by locality, of ordinary citizens in deciding spending priorities. This book examines how this democratic innovation works in practice and asks the difficult questions. Can local participation in public management really strengthen its efficiency? Is genuine participation possible without small groups monopolizing power? Can local organizations avoid becoming bureaucratized and cut off from their roots? Can neighborhood mobilization go beyond parochialism and act in the general interest? The book also raises the bigger question about what lessons can be learned from Porto Alegre to renew democratic institutions elsewhere in the world." Source: Presentation, Amazon site.

http://www.amazon.com/The-Porto-Alegre-Experiment-Democracy/dp/1842774050

(xii) Prefeitura de Guarulhos, **Guarulhos, vivencias e aprendizados. Orçamento Participativo,** 2008. 155 pp

A publicação conta a história da experiencia do Orçamento Participativo de Guarulhos para que "ela possa ser recontada, aprendida e transformada (...) estimule e fortaleça o exercício da práxis (ação- reflexão-ação) dos diversas sujeitos e atores sociais comprometidos com a as práticas participativas para a transformação das relações políticas não-democráticas que ainda pautam a nossa sociedade do século 21". Um documento para refletir sobre o muito que ainda temos a aprender com a América Latina, em especial através do exemplo de Guarulhos no Brasil.

http://siteantigo.paulofreire.org/pub/Crpf/CrpfAcervo000139/Legado_Prefeitura_Guarulhos_
Orcamento_Participativo.pdf

(xiii) Salinas Fernández, Juan (comp). **Ciudadanos transformando ciudades: el presupuesto participativo de la Serena, Chile. Participación Ciudadana Activa en los**

Espacios Locales. Municipalidad de La Serena. 2012, 168 pp

Interesante sistematización reflexiva e informativa de la experiencia de La Serena, en Chile. Después de elementos de contexto, en particular sobre la participación ciudadana, se presenta el programa a partir de la varias delegaciones que componen el municipio, dando la voz a los protagonistas. La recopilación incluye el innovador presupuesto participativo escolar, dando la voz a los estudiantes. Concluye sobre una decena de hitos que dan a la experiencia su carácter único tales como, la escuela participativa de liderazgo social, la formación de los funcionarios, la metodología de cartografía social, o el sistema informático sustentando el proceso.

http://issuu.com/laserena/docs/libro_pp_la_serena

(xiv) Sousa Santos, Boaventura de. **Democracia y participación. El ejemplo del presupuesto participativo.** ILDIS-FES, Abya Yala, Quito, 2004, 269 pp

El libro describe brevemente el contexto político brasileño y las principales instituciones y procesos vinculados al presupuesto participativo de Porto Alegre desde su surgimiento. Se analiza el presupuesto participativo en función de su eficacia redistributiva, la calidad de la participación, la autonomía del proceso frente al Ejecutivo y las tensiones existentes entre democracia participativa y democracia representativa. Apunta, según su autor, a definir la contribución del Presupuesto Participativo a la reinvención de la democracia, examinando sus potencialidades y los límites para su universalización, como principio organizativo de una forma de gobierno municipal democrática y redistributiva.

http://ilsa.org.co:81/node/52

C – Evaluations

(xv) Asterina, N, Hidayani, R, Rifai, A, **Improving the transparency, inclusivity and impact of participatory budgeting in Indonesian cities,** Kota Kita a city for all, Program Making all voices count, 2016, 84 pp

Kota Kita is an Indonesian civil society organization that focuses on urban planning and citizen participation. They led a pioneering participatory budgeting process in the city of Solo. At the same time Kota Kita has been heavily involved in the organization of various Indonesian Social Forum, addressing key urban issues with social movements and the civil society. In this research they explore [a] the current status of participatory budgeting in six Indonesian cities within a participatory planning and budgeting context known as *Musrenbang*, [b] the barriers and enablers to implementing participatory budgeting. It provides interesting recommendations for both national and local governments on how the *Musrenbang* and PB process can be improved.

http://www.kotakita.org/library

(xvi) Fedozzi, Luciano, **Observando o OP de Porto Alegre, perfil social e associativo, avaliação, formação de uma cultura política democrática e possíveis inovações,** 2009, Ed Observa POA, 138 pp

A partir de um material riquíssimo e único se apresenta com gráficos e tabelas comentadas a evolução do perfil do público que participa nas assembleias regionais e temáticas do Orçamento Participativo de Porto Alegre. Os dados apresentados auxiliam a necessária reflexão sobre o funcionamento dos mecanismos de participação, e passados 20 anos desde o seu lançamento demostra, a pesar do seus limites, a importância de este mecanismo de participação cidadã.

http://lproweb.procempa.com.br/pmpa/prefpoa/observatorio/usu_doc/livro_op_digital.pdf

(xvii) Martínez, Carlos R, Arena Emiliano, **Experiencias y buenas prácticas en presupuesto participativo, Fondo de las Naciones Unidas para la Infancia (UNICEF),** Buenos Aires, 2013, 108 pp

"En el Capítulo 1, se presenta al PP como una política destinada a fortalecer la democracia. Se refiere brevemente el origen de esta política y su historia y difusión actual en Argentina. El Capítulo 2 da cuenta de la sistematización de experiencias de presupuesto

participativo en Argentina a través del análisis de variables especialmente seleccionadas. Tras este exhaustivo desarrollo, el Capítulo 3 reúne las buenas prácticas encontradas en las experiencias relevadas. Con especial énfasis, el Capítulo 4 aborda la participación ciudadana de niños, adolescentes y jóvenes, destacando la importancia de promover las buenas prácticas para la integración de esta población". Fuente: Resumen publicación.

http://www.unicef.org/argentina/spanish/monitoreo_sistematizacion_PresupuestoParticipativo.pdf

(xviii) Torres Ribeiro A.; Gracia, G. **Participatory Budget trial. From 1997 – 2000.** Fórum Nacional de Participacão Popular, Oxfam, Editora Vozes, Petrópolis, 2002, 120 pp

This is the first, extensive, systematic assessment of Brazilian Participatory Budgeting experiences, conducted by the National Forum for Popular Participation. It is essential for understanding the diversity of this method developed in over a hundred cities in Brazil from 1997 to 2000. It includes synthesis and a detailed record, organised into tables, of PB experiences, and remains an exceptional overview of the diversity of participatory budgeting in Brazil. Published originally in Portuguese in 2003, Editora Vozes.

D - Manuals, legal tools and methods

(xix) **Ayuntamiento de Sevilla, Autorreglamento Presupuestos Participativos 2008.** 2010, 24 pp

Publicação do Município de Sevilha com todos os documentos oficiais normativos e legais do Orçamento Participativo desta cidade entre 2008 e 2010. Uma referência única no contexto dos Orçamentos Participativos Europeus.

http://participacion.ayto-caceres.es/files/auto%20reglamento%20sevilla.pdf

(xx) Associação in loco; Câmara Municipal de São Brás de Alportel; Agrupamento vertical de Escolas de São Brás de Alportel; Escola secundária José Belchior Viegas. **Orçamento participativo Crianças e Jovens Manual de Recurso.** 2012, 82 pp

Especialmente vocacionado para o público jovem, o documento começa com uma reflexão geral sobre a crise das democracias liberais e a necessidade de aprofundar as práticas de participação dos cidadãos como estratégia para a qualificação do regime. Reúne depois alguns elementos síntese sobre a história e o conceito dos Orçamentos Participativos no mundo, particularmente na situação portuguesa e na experiência concreta de Orçamento Participativo desenvolvido em São Brás de Alportel com as crianças e jovens desse concelho. Um manual que se justifica ler e usar no desenvolvimento de Orçamentos Participativos jovens.

http://portugalparticipa.pt/upload_folder/table_data/a3daa5b1-2931-498d-992c-46df4b4e96b9/files/OP_crianca.pdf

(xxi) Cabannes, Yves (2004). **72 Frequently Asked Questions about Participatory Budgeting.** Nairobi, UN-HABITAT. 90 pp

"This publication is a must-read in terms of PB implementation in Latin America and will be a fundamental tool for CSOs, researchers and policymakers interested in implementing PB in their own countries". Source: Spotlight on Knowledge, op cit. *"The present Manual of Frequently Asked Questions intends to respond in a direct and practical way to the general question of how best to implement a Participatory Budget. The Manual is a key entry point to a broader Participatory Budgeting Toolkit, which is based on a collection of four types of useful resources for all those interested in adopting and adapting Participatory Budgeting in a particular context. These four components are closely inter-linked and have been organized in the following form: a) Digital Library; b) Set of technical and legal instruments; c) City Fact Sheets; and d) Resource Directory of people, organizations, contacts and websites".* Source: Overview from UN-HABITAT site. Available in English, French, Portuguese and Spanish, Italian, Arabic and Chinese [UN Habitat website]

http://unhabitat.org/publications/72-frequently-asked-questions-about-participatory-budgeting/

(xxii) Communes de Chefchaouen, Tétouan et Larache, Maroc & Diputación de Jaén, Espagne, **Charte de principes pour le budget participatif,** 2015, 6 pp

Quelques villes officialisent le budget participatif non pas avec des « auto-règlements » ou des décrets mais par des chartes : c'est le cas par exemple à Paris et au Maroc. Cette charte de principes co-signée par trois villes du Nord du Maroc est la première formalisation d'engagements municipaux pour la mise en place de budget participatif dans le pays. Elle s'inspire *«aux valeurs de la démocratie participative, conformément à l'article 139 de la constitution marocaine»* et a été reconnue par le Ministère de l'Intérieur. Après un série de préambules et de définition cette charte précise quels sont les objectifs du BP, les règles de participation, le cycle du BP, la gestion du cycle, les dispositifs pour faire des propositions, son financement, la communication aux citoyens, la reddition des comptes et l'évaluation. Cette charte reflète les engagements positifs pris par quelques communes, suite aux dynamiques citoyennes et changements survenus à la suite du printemps arabe. Elle constitue une source d'inspiration pour des villes désirant démarrer des budgets participatifs. La charte est disponible en français et en arabe.

(xxiii) Enda/Ecopop, UN-Habitat, sous la direction de Bachir Kanouté, **Le budget participatif en Afrique, Guide pour la formation en pays francophones,** Vol 1 Concepts et principes, 86 pp; Vol 2, Méthodes et approches, 2008, 92 pp

Ce guide est toujours d'actualité, dix années après son lancement. Le premier volume aborde de manière simple, illustrée et adaptée au contexte des villes africaines : [1] un introduction au BP et aux concepts de base, ainsi qu'une mise en perspective avec la décentralisation et la gouvernance; [2] un analyse des différentes dimensions du BP : participative, financière, normative, juridique, institutionnelle, territoriale, socio-économique et culturelle ; [3] une troisième partie explore les conditions de mise en œuvre. Le second volume détaille de manière didactique et illustrée les différentes étapes d'un BP conventionnel, là encore pour un contexte africain : [1] lancement du processus ; [2] Etat des lieux ; [3] Régulation interne et définition des règles ; [4] Diagnostic et définition des priorités ; [5] Formation des alliances et dialogues ; [6] Mise en œuvre du BP ; [7] suivi et évaluation de l'exécution. A noter que ce manuel existe également, dans des versions légèrement modifiées, en portugais pour les contextes lusophones et en anglais pour les contextes anglophones.

Access Vol 1 : http://unhabitat.org/books/le-budget-participatif-en-afrique-manuel-de-formation-pour-les-pays-francophone/

Vol 2 : http://unhabitat.org/books/le-budget-participatif-en-afrique-manuel-de-formation-pour-les-pays-francophone-volume-ii-methodes-et-approches/

(xxiv) Nguebou, Jules Dumas, **Manuel du budget participatif au Cameroun: concepts, méthodes et outils pour suivre la décentralisation et améliorer la gouvernance locale,** ASSOAL, édité par le CRDL, 2014, 146 pp

Depuis 2003, des expériences sont en cours au Cameroun. En 2014, on en comptait 51 réparties dans les 10 régions du pays. Le document replace le budget participatif comme outil de la décentralisation, en cours au Cameroun depuis la constitution de 1996. L'analyse du contexte et des budgets publics permet de replacer le budget participatif dans une démarche de gouvernance locale. Pour la mise en place d'un budget participatif, le manuel souligne l'importance du plaidoyer, l'identification d'un cas pratique, puis la nécessité d'arrêtés municipaux, de la formation de comités de coordination et d'animation... avant de réaliser les différentes étapes du cycle du budget participatif. On y trouve des informations sur les mécanismes de contrôle testés au Cameroun (voir notamment la partie dédiée au comité d'animation et développement et à l'observatoire des services publics). Enfin, le document aborde le rôle de la médiation comme une fonction essentielle du processus : 14 fonctions y sont précisées, en mettant l'accent sur l'attitude et en proposant des techniques d'animation, ainsi que des techniques de plaidoyer et lobbying. [Présentation réalisée par Periferia, 2017]

http://www.ungana.org/IMG/pdf/manuel_du_budget_participatif_au_cameroun-2014.pdf

(xxv) Ley Nacional de Perú - LEY No 28056. **Ley Marco del Presupuesto Participativo.**
Perú fue el primer país a votar una ley nacional, que obliga los gobiernos locales a introducir el presupuesto participativo. Un texto legal de referencia.

http://www.oas.org/juridico/spanish/per_res19.pdf

(xxvi) Prefeitura de Porto Alegre Regimento Interno, **Critérios Gerais, Técnicos e Regionais**, 2010/2011, 76 pp
Uma publicação de 76 páginas dedicadas apenas ao Regimento Interno do Conselho do Orçamento Participativo de Porto Alegre do qual foram impressos 40.000 exemplares. Demonstrativo da importância da experiência e do profissionalismo e rigor com que todo o processo é regulado. Referencia para outras experiências de Orçamento Participativo no mundo. O regimento interno é atualizado para cada edição e se recomenda examinar as modificações e adaptações ocorridas através dos anos.

http://lproweb.procempa.com.br/pmpa/prefpoa/op/usu_doc/pa002010-op_reg_int.pdf

Selection of films on participatory budgeting produced between 2002 and 2017

金开展 "阳光惠民培训" 现场会
镇董坪村开班仪式

PARTICIPATORY BUDGETING

FILE
22

RESOURCE FILES

Selection of films on participatory budgeting produced between 2002 and 2017

Authors
Cabannes, Yves
ycabanes@mac.com
Delgado, Cecília
cmndelgado@gmail.com

Date
8/2014
Update 4/2017

This selection of documentaries and fiction films appear in different languages and are commented on here in English. Various excellent references are not included if they are not easily accessible. This is primarily the case for earlier Brazilian experiences. Around 25 additional films of interest in different languages are proposed at the end of this chapter.

Languages

English: (0) Portugal and world wide; (i) PB Project in NYC, United States and (ii) Solo Kota Kita, Indonesia (subtitles in English); (iii) Cotacachi, Ecuador (DRD);

Spanish: (iii) Cotacachi (DRD), (Spanish VOST in English and French), (iv) Algo se mueve en Málaga, España; (v) El Hatillo, Venezuela; (vi) Las mujeres y el presupuesto participativo, la experiencia Montevideana, Uruguay;

French: (vii) Fissel, Sénégal, (viii) Budget Participatif Lycéen - Région Nord Pas de Calais, France; (ix) Tunisia, Sfax and Gabés; (x) Sud Kivu, Congo Democratic Republic;

Portuguese: (0) Portugal and world wide; (xi) Porto Alegre, Brasil (Portuguese and French), (xii) O que é o orçamento participativo, Guarulhos, Brasil ; (xiii) Portuguese National Participatory Budgeting, (xix) São Brás Alportel, OP Jovens, Portugal.

(0) A quiet revolution / Uma revolução tranquila A film written by Giovanni Allegretti & Pierre Stoeber, directed by Pierre Stoeber, 42', 2014, Portuguese with English subtitles → vimeo.com/94308484

The documentary by Pierre Stoeber and Giovanni Allegretti relates to the "OPtar" project, an action-research that the Centre of Social Studies of Coimbra University conducted between 2010 and 2013. Its aim is to give the floor to politicians, civil servants, researchers and citizens involved in co-deciding on municipal resources, so to help to define the concept of Participatory Budgeting, clarify its positive challenges and some contradictions or fragilities detected during the last decade of experiments travelling around the world. Portugal - the country in Europe with the higher rate of experiments - is taken as a metaphoric place to test some of these challenges and fragilities, using data and outcomes of the project, although voices and images from different continents mix in the documentary. The ambition of this medium-length film is to show how much important emotions are in making PB functioning, and how much these small experiments, although often limited to local contexts, are important to qualify and intensify our democratic regimes. [extract from documentary presentation] CC BY-ND Pierre Stoeber - Solid Production, pierre.stoeber@laposte.net / +33680464496

(i) PB Project in New York City 2012, 9'17
→ www.youtube.com/watch?v= PYwDEO oCN5M

A diverse group of people, Black, Hispanic, old young, address the question, 'What is a participatory budgeting?'. Gloria, a Participatory Budgeting participant, explains why empowerment through participation strengthens the whole community. Stacy, a resident, teacher and Participatory Budgeting participant, confirms her excitement at the possibly of being part of the solution, through people power, to mould her communities in the way that she wants. Following that, the floor is given to the students to speak about their needs: technology, security cameras and lighting, pothole repairs and more young women's leadership training.

The video ends with the Council member, Melissa, revealing the results of the participatory Budgeting. Simple but powerful – just listen to what people say!

(ii) Solo Kota Kita Indonesia, 2011, 4'31 → www.youtube.com/results?client=sa fari&rls=en&q=(Solo+Kota+Kita&oe=UTF-8&um= 1&ie=UTF-8&sa=N&tab=w1

This is an institutional and didactic video in which the annual participatory budgeting cycle in Solo – Indonesia, adopted by the Solo government is introduced. The purpose of the video is to promote citizen advocacy and participatory planning by empowering people by sharing information. The three-step method is well explained: 1) meeting with community groups and leaders to identify concerns and needs; 2) conveying information and data from a Geographic Information System to the community at the neighbourhood–level (smallest administrative level) followed by sharing information, including maps and neighbourhood profiles; 3) dissemination through training workshops.

Giving information is a low cost procedure. Having people participating and involved makes the investment appropriate and sustainable. Solo Kota Kita encourages others to replicate the experience.

(iii) Cotacachi, Unity in Diversity 2008, 25', Produced by DRD, Radically Democratize Democracy network

→ www.dailymotion.com/video/xfs1qf_cotacachi-1-l-unite-dans-la-diversite_travel + Can be ordered through Catherine Gegout, cathgegout@laposte.net

An excellent documentary on the participation experience in the Canton of Cotacachi, Ecuador that began in 1996 after a Quechua Otavaleño Indian was elected Mayor. The documentary focuses on unity within the cultural, political and ethnic diversity that distinguishes the Canton. The process began with extensive citizenship capacity building for residents of all ages and backgrounds. The training was adapted to the needs and interests of each group, their language – either Spanish or Quechua – and took into consideration the diversity of the group, recognising a high level of mistrust among the various ethnic groups, along with the significance of ancestral knowledge and ways of life rooted in Andean Indian tradition.

After this period of training, a Participatory Development Plan for the Canton was formulated and the participatory budgeting process was set up. This experience brought about profound change in the lives of the people of Cotacachi. [Exists in Spanish and English]

Spanish

(iv) Algo se mueve en Málaga 2011, 43' [Things are Moving in Malaga]
→ uciencia.uma.es/Videos/Algo-se-mueve-en-Malaga or in 5 parts on youtube + Part 1 www.youtube.com/watch?v=vAHmmiGI45g

This video showcases 10 of the 18 municipalities in the province of Malaga that have implemented participatory budgeting. It provides a voice to citizens, facilitators, technicians and politicians, who discuss the most valuable aspects of the process and the lessons learned. The material illustrates and invites us to reflect on a variety of issues: participatory democracy as a universal, self-regulating and binding process; the importance of disseminating, communicating and attracting people to the process; the need to try out alternatives and to learn from mistakes; the interest in female "empowerment", projecting the future through the present; the vision of the collective based on a group of individual opinions. The last image leaves us with the message: "Another world is possible, and it begins in the municipalities, through participation."

(v) Alcaldía de El Hatillo, Venezuela ¿Qué es el Presupuesto Participativo? 2014, 3'36 → www.youtube.com/watch?v=d9d85SqojAY

Lively short spot introducing PB methods and process to common citizens, in a country where PB is not that frequent. A professor explains quite clearly how it works!

(vi) Las mujeres y el presupuesto participativo, la experiencia Montevideana 2012, 9'20 [Women and participatory budgeting, the Montevidean Experience] → www.youtube.com/watch?v=c55EWTN9S6U

This video focuses on the reflections of municipal personnel. The city of

Montevideo serves as a backdrop for a discussion of the participatory budgeting experience. The video is somewhat limited in its portrayal of the role of the citizens, as well as the stages of the process, for example relationships with the zonal council and the commitments made by the municipal executive, which are distinctive trademarks of participatory budgeting in Montevideo. However, it is still an interesting video, as one of the few documentaries on participatory budgeting with a clear focus on gender.

French

(vii) Fissel 2008, 20'00, Produced by DRD, Radically Democratize Democracy network → Cannot be accessed for free through Internet + Can be ordered through Catherine Gegout, cathgegout@laposte.net

An excellent documentary produced, in French, by the DRD Network "Democratiser Radicalement la Démocratie". The film aims to show "how things work in the field". One of the interesting aspects of the documentary is to give a voice to men and women of all ages who explain, in their own words, all the various phases, challenges and problems they encounter. Fissel is one of the pioneering PB experiences in Africa and is the culmination of a long process of local training and capacity building, spearheaded in Africa by IED, Institute for Environment and Development.

(viii) Region Nord Pas de Calais 2012, 5'00
→ www.youtube.com/watch?v= tFvMoGBdnOo

A short film that gives voice to school representatives, students, teachers, technical staff and principals. However the voice of parents who are also involved in the decision-making process is missing from the film. The Participatory Budgeting process in Secondary Schools focuses on providing equipment needed to improve quality of life and spans two years: In Year 1, the schools submit project proposals; in Year 2, the two or three projects selected are implemented.

(ix) Documentaire sur le processus du Budget Participatif en Tunisie

2015, Directed by Agence Local & Global, 23', In Arabic and sub-titles in French → www.youtube.com/watch?v=zUAmHTBLaHw

After a first round of experiments in 2014 in the Tunisian cities of La Marsa, Menzel Bourguiba and Tozeur, PB expanded to Sfax, Manouba and Gafsa in 2015. This remarkable documentary, shot primarily in Sfax and Gafsa provides an insiders' view to the first significant PB experiences in the Arab world. It illuminates the roles of civil society organizations and some its key players such as Kouraich Jaouahdou in breaking new grounds for participation and local democracy. The documentary highlights the importance of information, communication and media coverage to open up new forms of dialogue with local governments and among citizens, in which women and the youth gained legitimacy and are playing a determining role.

(x) Le budget Participatif, une réalité au Sud-Kivu

République Démocratique du Congo, directed 3 TAMIS, Centre de production video participative, Bukavu, Sud Kivu for PRCG [Projet de Renforcement des Capacités en Gouvernance], 2013, 32'33

→ www.youtube.com/watch?v= Qtu1xZWCoT0

This documentary film shows the very first steps of participatory budgeting in villages and small towns from Kivu, on the aftermath of political turmoil and armed conflicts. What is unique about the situation shown is that elections at local governments level still do not exist in the country and PB is being implemented despite the lack of decentralised elected governments with full responsibilities and budgetary resources. The experience demonstrates that PB can become a reality even in dire financial situations and can contribute to peace making, turning "another possible world" a reality.

(xi) Porto Alegre. La ville est à nous, 2000, 27'46, Emission Sagacités n°319 sur le budget participatif de Porto Alegre [in Portuguese and French] → www.dailymotion.com/video/x20t0yo_la-ville-est-a-nous-emission-sagacites-sur-le-budget-participatif-de-porto-alegre_webcam

This is a rare film from the earlier times of PB that captures the energy and creativity of the period. It documents participatory budget in the city where it all started in 1989. And advocates for citizenship as a learning process based on direct decision-making by communities for collective well-being. The video addresses in detail most phases of the process and gives voice to the people, community leaders as well as local authorities representatives.

(xii) O que é o Orçamento Participativo Guarulhos, 2009, 8'14 [What is Participatory Budgeting?] → www.youtube.com/watch?v=2aJHRmwJOMM

How can you manage the household budget using the participatory budgeting methodology? Taking one family as an example, the mother, children and grandmother discuss the household and individual priorities as the base of the collective budget. Then the aunt arrives – the neighbourhood representative in the Participatory Budgeting Council – to remind the head of household – the mother – of the meeting to be held on that day. With this pretext, the participatory budgeting cycle is explained, and the roles of the citizens and the elected representatives. After the meeting, back in the family room, the household budget is decided on, following the participatory budgeting model: cut back in current expenses to do larger products, prioritize the collective interest over individual wants. This form of alternative communication in a domestic setting, is an attempt to bring the discursive language closer to the popular context.

(xiii) Orçamento Participativo Portugal 2017, 2'26
→ www.youtube.com/watch?v=eqC7cYzPYPE

This short announcement is selected here simply because it invites Portuguese citizens to participate in the first ever participatory budgeting at national level that will start in 2017. Resources are still quite limited but it certainly opens up a new era for PB.

(xix) São Brás, OP Jovens 2009, 2'30

→ www.youtube.com/watch?v=gYIofumS_YM

This video was produced by a group of young students who document various problems within the context of the school that are begging to be addressed: repairing the pipes in the bathrooms, damaged shutters, missing lockers, deteriorated sports fields and green spaces, irregular car parking obstructing the path ways, etc. It is a young and innocent video that demonstrates that it is possible, with limited technological resources, to communicate the needs and expectations of young people in an impactful way.

Other films of interest available on Internet

English

1. City view: Participatory Budgeting in Cambridge, United Kingdon, 2016, 4'51
→ www.youtube.com/watch?v=fZS48720gwg

2. Participatory Budgeting in Edinburgh, 2016, 5'31
→ www.youtube.com/watch?v=WCOgwDuCUlM

3. Improving Rural Life through Participatory Budgeting - The Ekiti Success Story, Nigeria, 2016, 10'47
→ www.youtube.com/watch?v =SZcuMfPrODY

4. Real Money, Real Power, Participatory Budgeting Project, USA, 2013, 4'13
→ council.nyc.gov/pb/

5. Participatory Budgeting in Chicago's 49th Ward, 2012, 5'38
→ www.youtube.com/watch?v=oe-nbxsmjYw

6. Toronto Community Housing Participatory Budgeting, 2009, 3'
→ www.youtube.com/watch?v=mi7EeSO_r_o

Spanish

7. Presupuestos Participativos 2017 de Zaragoza # Construye TuBarrio, 2016, 1'28"
→ www.youtube.com/watch?v=gC7929AbVIO

8. Presupuestos Participativos. Usaquen 2014, Bogotá, Colombia
→ www.youtube.com/watch?v=4NjtryO6OCE

9. Vecinos votan por Presupuestos Participativos 2010, La Serena, Chile, 2'18
→ www.youtube.com/watch?v=iUQHbGtyoGc

10. Spot presupuesto participativo, Ilo , Peru, 2010, 0'33
→ www.youtube.com/watch?v=QHTeMGtvCA8

11. Seville, Spain. Asambleas de presupuestos participativos en 2010
→ www.youtube.com/watch?v=cDcRJMh4uqI

12. Entregan patrullas y motocicletas en Iztapalapa, México, 2013, 2'42
→ www.youtube.com/watch?v=hLLwlmtz4-A

French

14. Le budget Participatif 2016, comment ça marche? La Mairie du 15e vous explique tout en 4 minutes [existe pour chaque arondissement]
→ budgetparticipatif.paris.fr/bp/jsp/site/Portal.jsp?document_id=2253&portlet_id=171

15. Réel argent, pouvoir réel: le budget participatif, by The Participatory Budgeting Project, . 2014, 3'26 [anglais, sous-titré en français]
→ www.youtube.com/watch?v=YByJwJQPeg4

16. Ideal EU, Poitou - Charentes, France, 2008, 7'40
→ www.youtube.com/watch?v=nkxhgAippTI

17. Tirage au sort de conseils de quartier pour voter les budgets, Grigny, France, 2012, 11'46"
→ http://www.youtube.com/watch?v=2O7eNdCgiss

18. Budget Participatif Lycéen, Nord Pas-de-Calais, France. Participation du Domaine agricole de Radinghem, 2011, 2'25
→ www.youtube.com/watch?v=p4Z6oooLfKs

19. Budget participatif, Ampasy Nahampoana, Madagascar, 2012, 6'54
→ www.youtube.com/watch?v=8QSF3wPpFxU&feature=youtu.be

Portuguese

20. Aldeia participativa. Sá-Monção, Portugal, 2011, 2'50
→ www.youtube.com/watch?v=Xly6gRcralA

21. Orçamento participativo Mirim, 2016, Santo André
→ www.youtube.com/watch?v=H9Os3LQBV7k

22. Orçamento Participativo faz 10 anos em Guarulhos, Brasil, 2010, WebTV
→ www.youtube.com/watch?v=nGP6nHcfVQo ;

24. Orçamento Participativo, Lisboa, Portugal, 2012, 2'55
→ www.youtube.com/watch?v=La7pjxmdAe8

25. Orçamento Participativo 2011, Porto Alegre, Brazil, 2011
→ www.youtube.com/watch?v=_HCLDbpcSn0

26. Prefeitura Araraquara, Orçamento Participativo, Brasil, 2017
→ www.youtube.com/watch?v=XSh5fzJnxqQ

Websites on Participatory Budgeting

Websites on Participatory Budgeting

Authors
Cabannes, Yves
ycabanes@mac.com
Delgado, Cecília
cmndelgado@gmail.com

Date
03/2014
Update 4/2017

This selection of commented on PB websites mirrors the different scales they usually cover:

Supra-national: International observatory of Participatory Democracy; Budgeting and Gender in Latin America and the Caribbean; Periferia

National: Brazilian Participatory Budgeting Network, Brazil; Chilean Participatory Budgeting Network, Chile; The Participatory Budgeting Project, North America; Portugal Participa, Portugal; Buergerhaushalt, Germany

Municipal: Paris, France; Rosario, Argentina and Medellin, Colombia

Infra-municipal [Wards, Districts, Parishes, Arrondissements]: Chicago 49th Ward, USA

This short sample of commented upon websites is complemented with a second selection of 20 others that are worth consulting. The table below indicates the websites working languages:

PARTICIPATORY BUDGETING
FILE
23
RESOURCE FILES

	English	French	Spanish	Portuguese	German
SUPRA-NATIONAL	(i) (ii)	(i) (ii) (iii)	(i) (ii)	(i) (ii)	
NATIONAL	(vi) (viii)	(iii)	(v)	(iv) (vii)	(viii)
MUNICIPAL		(ix)	(x) (xi)		
INFRA-MUNICIPAL	(xii)				

268

(i) International Observatory on Participatory Democracy (OIDP): https://www.oidp.net/pt/

Provides information on its work, especially the "Best Practice in Citizen Participation" Award, and the Local Observatory on Participatory Democracy. Includes a diverse Resource Center: library, media, case studies (on participatory budgeting and other issues), methodological guidelines, etc. One standout feature is the constant dissemination of information on relevant upcoming events. Based in Barcelona, the network has been in place since 2006, in partnership with organizations like United Cities and Local Governments.

(ii) Budgeting and Gender in Latin America and the Caribbean: http://www.presupuestoygenero.net

Explains the basic concepts behind gender-sensitive participatory budgeting, provides documentation, guidelines and manuals, as well a other complementary literature. Offers a database of specialists in the issue. Provides a space and a voice to women protagonists through videos and testimonies encompassing various Latin American Countries. Also offers news, event information, and newsletters produced by the platform.

(iv) Periferia: http://periferia.be/index.php/fr/archives-fr/base-de-donnees

This recent and well organized site is primarily an information databank of documents and films organized along the following: [1] References that explain which are the essential PB principles and that clarify the key steps important to consider in a PB process; [2] Information on PB experiments implemented at regional, city or district levels; [3] Analytical documents and research reports drawing lessons from experiences. Most of the documents are in French and can be downloaded for free. The non-profit social enterprise, Periferia, that manages this site is based in

FILE 23 · WEBSITES

Belgium and therefore provides specialized information on current PB processes implemented in the country, such as Scheut or Saint Josse, in which they are or have been engaged in.

National Level

(v) **Brazilian Participatory Budgeting Network, Rede OP Brasil:** http://www.redeopbrasil.com.br

Provides general information on Participatory Budgeting, especially on Latin America and Brazil. Provides access to some documents in English, Spanish and French. Given that Brazil is a global benchmark in Participatory Budgeting, it is an essential site. The exclusive use of Portuguese makes it difficult to share experiences with non-Portuguese speakers.

(vi) **Chilean Participatory Budgeting Forum:** www.presupuestoparticipativo.cl/FORO

Provides news, documents, photos, videos, and links on municipalities that are members of the Chilean Participatory Budgeting network. Includes an interesting link on answers to frequently asked questions. Experts in the field support the network.

(vii) **The Participatory Budgeting Project, North America:** http://www.participatorybudgeting.org

The Participatory Budgeting Project started in 2005 between a group of activists and researchers based in the United State and Canada. It's a non-profit organization that works on the empowerment of community members on Participatory Budgeting process. The site is the front screen of the organization allowing them to catch public attention simultaneously with public education. Some of the more frequently asked questions are answered through the site: what is a PB; where has it worked; how to participate. There is also a resource toolbox with examples of others

Participatory Budgeting experiences, videos, photos, etc. Easy to navigate through and excellent references on United States.

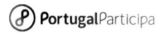 **(viii) Portugal Participa, Rede de autarquias participativas:** http://www. portugalparticipa.pt

Managed by the Portuguese In Loco Association in partnership with some Portuguese Local Governments , the site acts as an observatory and a resource center for learning about PB processes in Portugal, as well as providing access to information on some experiences in Latin America and Europe through the *Banco de Experiências* link. It has a vast and interesting library of international documents on participatory budgeting, from which visitors can download publications, manuals, guides, articles, etc., available in various languages. The "National Observatory" section encourages collaboration by sharing information on new experiences in participatory budgeting. Given the variety of information and the constant updates, it is a site worth visiting regularly.

 **(ix) Germany - Buergerhaushalt.org:** http://buergerhaushalt.de/en

German's online portal for participatory budgeting and related issues. The site enables anyone to obtain primarily information on participatory budgeting in Germany. Users can also obtain practical tips and materials for implementing Participatory Budgeting, and benefit from the lessons learned by other practitioners. It provides an English version of the website with a selection of texts from the German version. It is the best way to stay in touch, and up-to-date on German Participatory Budgeting.

Municipal / City based

 **(x) Paris, France** (see file 16): https://budget participatif.paris.fr/bp/

Paris Participatory Budgeting *[Budget Participatif]* site offers what you should expect to participate in a PB process and be kept well informed about PB in your city. As it is organized it tremendously helps to turn the process transparent and this probably explains the growing success PB Paris has enjoyed through its short three years existence. It offers key sections:

[i] *Basic information* on Paris Budget: how does it works, presentation of the Charter that gives details on who can participate; what are the eligible projects; how you can participate; the various steps trough which projects are selected; a calendar; etc. Downloading of a communication kit containing the PB charter; a PB flyer; visual basic information or accessing short videos is an easy task.

[ii] The site is as well an *interactive platform* that allows citizens to make proposal and suggest ideas that will be developed, discussed upon and voted during the PB cycle. It allows as well people to ask questions that will be answered on a one to one basis.

[iii] The section dedicated to projects *follow up* gives a snapshot of the degree of implementation of projects that were approved in recent years and whether they were inaugurated or not. Access to project implementation can be done through the year they were voted, the issue they address or the district where they are implemented.

One could expect in the future more information on PB experiments worldwide and a digital library for those who want to go further. Additional data and pictures on the projects under implementation or already implemented could be quite useful as well.

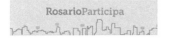

(xi) Rosario, Argentina (see file 10): https://participa.rosario.gob.ar

Participatory budgeting *[presupuesto participativo]* is hosted within Rosario Local Government website. Easy to navigate, with over 13 000 references on PB, this site has been regularly upgraded and improved over the last 15 years since PB was introduced in the city. It provides updated information on current PB processes and outcomes, and gives the list of the projects approved for each one of the districts. Detailed districts maps locate most of 1700 projects that were implemented since 2002. One could have expected a more detailed description of each project as well as a rate of advancement for the more recent ones that are at implementation stage. It enjoys a good digital library with [1] downloadable basic tools [guidelines, criteria for selection of projects, manual, etc.]; [2] crucial information on the PB processes and outcomes for each years and some evaluations. We particularly liked the dictionary on PB that is part of a laudable effort to turn PB specialized jargon more understandable to citizens. It is probably the only one existing so far; [c] Additional research and early references from other cities complement the library. In summary one excellent example of a city based site on PB.

MEDELLÍN DIGITAL
www.medellindigital.gov.co

(xiv) Medellin Digital, Colombia: http://www.medellindigital.gov.co

Medellin Digital is a program of the Municipality of Medellin, which uses new technologies as a tool for interaction – especially targeted to young people. A quick search brings visitors to the participatory budgeting page, which provides the necessary information to understand the process: what it is, the methodology followed; why vote, where to vote, and contacts. It has the huge value added of serving as a blog, allowing for interaction among users who can leave their comments and link them to Facebook and Twitter. A cutting-edge way of spreading the message of participatory budgeting through digital technology, in a language appropriate and attractive to young citizens.

Infra municipal level [Districts, wards, parishes & arrondissement]

(xiii) Chicago, Ward 49th United States (see file 4): http://www.ward49.com/participatory-budgeting/

Through recent years, some districts and wards are inserting their PB experiments within their site, or designing dedicated web sites that mirror what is happening in turn of the process and approved projects. This is for instance, the case in 49th Ward, Chicago described in the book (see file

4] or in France [*arrondissement*] and Portugal [*juntas de freguesias*].

The site is clear and organized along quite simple entries: [a] recent and past projects updates. Detailed location maps at Ward scale allow visualizing where the works approved through PB are located. It therefore helps residents to verify in situ changes that occurred; [b] introduction and presentation of PB that is entering its 8th cycle in 2017; [c] elections results in previous years; [d] FAQ about PB in the 49th Ward. An interesting section on " what others are saying about PB" complements the site. The site is essentially for local residents and is both in English and Spanish, as part of the population of the Ward and Chicago as a whole are of Latin American origins. Here is a good example of what can be done at local level to contribute to PB transparency in an inclusionary perspective.

Other valuable websites on PB

Supra-national

1. International Budget Partnership, United States: **http://www.internationalbudget.org**

2. Budget Participatif info [in French]: **https://budgetparticipatif.info/?cat=4**

National

3. France, Les Budgets Participatifs: **http://lesbudgetsparticipatifs.fr**

4. Peru, Perú Ministerio de Economía y Finanzas: **https://www.mef.gob.pe/es/presupuesto-participativo**

5. Scotland, Participatory Budgeting Scotland: **https://pbscotland.scot**
6. Spain, Red por los Presupuestos Participativos la Democracia Económica la Planificación Democrática: **http://www.ciudadesparticipativas.eu**
7. United Kingdom, Making People Count. PB Network: **https://pbnetwork.org.uk/category/geographic/international/_**

Municipal

8. Belo Horizonte, Brazil: **http://portalpbh.pbh.gov.br/pbh/ecp/comunidade.do?app=portaldoop**
9. Buffalo, United States: **http://www.pbbuffalo.org**
10. Cambridge, United kingdom: **http://pb.cambridgema.gov**
11. Cascais, Portugal: **http://op.cascaisparticipa.pt/orcamento-participativo**
12. Gijón, Spain: **http://transparencia.gijon.es/page/16285-presupuesto-participativo-2017**
13. Lisboa, Portugal: **http://www.lisboaparticipa.pt/pages/orcamentoparticipativo.php**
14. Montevideo, Uruguay: **http://presupuestoparticipativo.montevideo.gub.uy**
15. ntreuil, France: **http://www.montreuil.fr/vie-citoyenne/le-budget-participatif/**

16. New York, United States: **http://council.nyc.gov/pb/**
17. North Ayrshire, Scotland: **http://www.northayrshire.community/get-involved/participatory-budgeting-in-north-ayrshire/**
18. Porto Alegre, Brazil: **http://www2.portoalegre.rs.gov.br/op/**
19. Quillota, Chile: **https://www.quillota.cl/web/sitio/?p=21847**
20. Rennes, France: **http://fabriquecitoyenne.rennes.fr**
21. Toronto, Canada: **https://www.torontohousing.ca/residents/getting-involved/participatory-budgeting**

Infra-municipal [Districts, Junta de Freguesias, Arrondissements]

22. Junta de Freguesia de Castelo Branco, Castelo Branco, Portugal: **http://www.opfcb.pt**
23. 12º Arrondissement, Paris, France: **http://www.mairie12.paris.fr/mairie12/jsp/site/Portal.jsp?page_id=576**

List of the contributors

Barbara Lipietz is a Lecturer at the Bartlett's Development Planning Unit, University College London where she co-directs the MSc in Urban Development Planning and convenes the Research Cluster on Urban Transformations. Barbara's research interests center on urban governance, participatory governance and planning through co-production. She is particularly interested in – and actively supports – alternatives to competitive and 'world city' agendas, including mobilizations towards the 'just city', the 'right to the city' or 'liveable cities'. Barbara also has a keen interest in the pedagogy for community-led strategic action planning.

Cecília Delgado is a Portuguese Post-doctoral and Urban Planner and Architect with extensive experience as a University Lecturer and Researcher. Cecília specializes in participatory methods and innovations in urban planning, urban agriculture policies, and gendered urbanism. Currently she is part of CICS. NOVA, Interdisciplinary Centre of Social Sciences, at Nova University, Lisbon, where she works as a researcher on public policies. Cecília's current fields of research include land use planning, urban and peri-urban agriculture, and social inclusion.

Christopher Yap is a Doctoral Researcher and Participatory Video-Maker at the Centre for Agroecology, Water and Resilience, Coventry University. His research explores the relationships between urban agriculture, food sovereignty and the right to the city. Christopher has previously worked at the Bartlett Development Planning Unit, University College London, and the London International Development Centre, conducting action- and policy-oriented research on urban agriculture and urban development planning in the global North and South, as well as the post-2015 development agenda. Christopher holds an MSc Development Administration and Planning from University College London.

Hugo González Franetovic is a Community Psychologist and Social Planner. Between 2006 and 2009 Hugo worked as Municipal Delegate in one of the most vulnerable territories in La Serena, Chile. From 2009 to 2012 he coordinated the Community Participatory Budgeting Program through its first period, and he reassumed the role in January 2016. He has extensive experience in community work and psycho-social intervention with vulnerable urban and rural groups in diverse regions, communes, neighborhoods, territories, organizations and families. For almost 20 years Hugo has worked in participatory planning and evaluation of participatory programs, projects and processes.

Juan Salinas Fernández is a Social Worker and Master in Social Policies and Regional and Local Management with extensive experience in design and implementation of participatory programs within the Chilean municipal administration, particularly participatory budgeting processes at the municipal level. Juan is Adviser to local authorities and management teams on the implementation of the main participatory budgeting programs under development in Chile. He is also currently a member of the technical department at the Chilean Association of municipalities, an entity intended to provide technical assistance and support to the 345 Municipalities in Chile, particularly on processes of participatory planning.

Lenira Rueda Almeida is a Sociologist from Federal University of Minas Gerais and Specialist in Public Management at University of Campinas with experience in participatory public policies. Lenira is author of "Homens em Série - a história de Ipatinga contada por seus próprios personagens", in two volumes, as well as articles on participatory budgeting, social participation and participatory methodologies for basic sanitation planning. Lenira currently works in the Administration of Minas Gerais State with Regional Government Forums to promote social dialogue between local municipalities. She worked in the Regional Engineering and Agronomy Council of Minas Gerais in the development of a participatory training methodology in Municipal Basic Sanitation Plans. Lenira has conducted consultancy for Belo Horizonte City Hall and the Northwest Regional Secretariat in Participatory Budgeting, Housing and Planning, and worked as Advisor for Housing, Social Work, Women, Children and Young Adults in Belo Horizonte.

Millaray Carrasco Reyes is a Commercial Engineer at the University of La Serena, Chile, and Master in Public and Local Management and Administration from Menéndez Pelayo and Carlos III International University of Madrid, Spain. Millaray holds diplomas in Quality Management, Local Government and Development, Integrated Municipal Quality Management, Participatory Planning and Territorial Management, among others. She is a Lead Auditor in Integrated Management Systems, formerly Internal Auditor ISO 9001 (2008), and Accredited Evaluator of the UIM Model for Good Governance and Democratic Quality. For 12 years Millaray has worked in the Municipality of La Serena, Chile, in charge of the Municipal Budget, Transparency and Participatory Budgeting. She is currently the Coordinator of the Municipal Quality Management Program, within which has been coordinating the implementation of continued improvements within the Municipality of La Serena since 2008 and is part of the Executive Secretariat of Municipalities Twinning for Quality in Chile.

Yves Cabannes is a Planner and Urban Specialist. Since the mid 1990's he has been involved in research, implementation, teaching, and advocacy on participatory budgeting in a large number of countries and was Senior Advisor to the Municipality of Porto Alegre, Brazil, for the international network on participatory budgeting. Yves has published extensively on participatory budgeting and local alternatives for people-led development. He is committed to civil society initiatives in different regions and a member of the board of various foundations and social economy initiatives. Yves is Emeritus Professor of Development Planning, formerly Chair of Development Planning [2006-2015], at the Bartlett Development Planning Unit (DPU), University College London. He was previously Lecturer in Urban Planning at Harvard University Graduate School of Design and the Regional Coordinator of the UN-Habitat/UNDP Urban Management Program for Latin America and the Caribbean from 1997 to 2004. He has worked for many years with local governments, NGOs and social movements in various countries, primarily Mexico, Brazil and Ecuador.